Dogs, Donkeys and Circus Performers

Janine Jacques, mba, mscis, ph.d

Service Dog Project, Inc.
Training Dogs for the Mobility Impaired

DEDICATION
To the Service Dog Project
Changing lives & Making a difference

Janine Jacques

ACKNOWLEDGMENTS

Thank you to all of the animals that made this book possible and filled my life with purpose, entertainment and love.

Thank you also to all the followers of the Service Dog Project, Equine Rescue Network and Explore.org. Without you, progress and momentum would not be possible..

INDEX

PREFACE

This is a story of my family fortune and how we manage our enormous personal wealth.

How we define wealth in my family is perhaps different from most. We define wealth in terms of what we have accomplished and our ability to combine hard-work, creativity and energy for the benefit of others. By this definition, my family is wealthy. Very wealthy, perhaps sitting on a virtual goldmine – a fortune that is limitless as our family tree expands and lessons on wealth management are passed on to future generations.

Only a life lived for others is a life worthwhile. *Albert Einstein.*

If our wealth was defined by our material possessions, we might be placed firmly in the middle class. However, in taking measure of our material wealth, we include our valued possessions, the animals that share our lives. How can their worth be measured? This motley crew of rescue animals won't appear on any balance sheet yet has enriched our lives for years.

By our family's definition of wealth, the Service Dog Project (SDP) is probably the most valuable asset in our family's wealth portfolio. An enormous amount of hard work, creativity and energy has gone into creating the SDP, a nonprofit organization that provides service dogs to benefit people with mobility problems. It is an amazing and unique program that has made our family rich with accomplishments and has benefited many others.

The Service Dog Project (SDP) is one of 1.4 million registered 501C(3) nonprofit organizations in the United States. Yet, anyone who visits the SDP farm in Ipswich, Massachusetts will attest, it is like no other place on earth. Recently webcams were installed around the farm so that people from afar can experience the daily escapades online. The virtual experience delights people keeping them glued to their electronic screens. It seems everyone wants to know the origins of such a unique place. But there is no simple answer. It is a long, ongoing story of animal adventures, creativity, and lessons learned.

I know the SDP story well because it parallels the story of my life. Carlene White, the founder of the SDP, is also my mother. I refer to her not as "Mom or Mother" but simply as "Carlene."

I am the founder of the Equine Rescue Network, an organization that rescues horses from slaughter. One family, founding two sustainable nonprofit organizations is no coincidence.

Carlene and I have a bit of a strange relationship. It is definitely not the usual mother/daughter relationship. Rather, our relationship extends to include friendship, loyalty and a bit of fear. We are from the same gene pool and share what I refer to as the "Crazy Carlene Gene."

The Crazy Carlene Gene is not exclusive to our family tree. As you read the adventures of the animals of "Crazy Acres," you will see that this "Crazy Carlene Gene" manifests itself in people outside of our family as well. People who have this gene are innovative, enthusiastic and have the ability to laugh their way through many of life's biggest challenges. They all value their own internal wealth the same as my family does: wealth is about what you have done and how your actions have benefited others. In fact, perhaps it's not a gene after all, but a mindset that can be acquired and shared. If more people were to adopt the "Crazy Carlene Gene" and calculate wealth as we do, I suspect the world would be a better place – especially for the animals.

This book tells the story of the offbeat real life accomplishments and hard work scenarios that built our family's wealth. In it, I hope readers will find lessons that will help them assess and manage their own personal wealth as my family has. Regardless, I promise to at least entertain you with the animal adventures that led to the origins of the Service Dog Project and the Equine Rescue Network. The stories are all true – No imagination could possibly make this stuff up! So let us start at the beginning...

1. EARLY DAYS

I was born in 1965 into what appeared a normal family; Carlene (my mother) was a lovely woman, my father was a dashing physician. Our home was a peaceful 20-acre New England farm. Yet looking closer, you would find that looks can be deceiving. My father was not actually my biological father. I would later learn that Carlene had been married to another man, an alcoholic. One night, the alcoholic came home drunk and proceeded to argue abusively with Carlene in the kitchen. He lunged at her in a drunken rage. To protect herself, she grabbed the nearest thing, a frying pan. One swing and the man fell to the floor. Carlene hadn't intended to inflict harm but she had two young children protect and no time to live a life of domestic abuse. Fearing that he might be even angrier when he woke up, she dragged him into the kitchen pantry and locked the door. She called the doctor and explained what happened. That was back in the day when doctors made house calls. Dr. Thomas White arrived a short time later. My biological father was not dead. Carlene had his things packed by the time he emerged from the closet a bit groggy with a pounding headache. In due course, Dr. White moved in. I was so young; he was the only father I ever knew.

Dr White was a general practitioner in our small town, strikingly handsome with a gregarious bedside manner. He was revered as a professional and considered a "heart throb" to all the women in town. And he did seem to understand the nature of his new wife, as he gave her a baby piglet for their first anniversary. Carlene had forgotten it was even their anniversary but was so pleased with the piglet and eager to start its training. The piglet, given the name Lucy, was not a miniature pig and soon grew to 500 pounds. She loved people and was very smart - often too smart. She learned to walk on a leash, sit, stay and fetch. At meal time Lucy sat with us at a specially designed table. She was a lovely pet, yet she still was a pig and her snout often got busy on the flowerbeds.

My father enjoyed a nicely run, well landscaped home and Lucy was often working against him; eating flowers, digging up bushes, and making mud-baths in his manicured lawn. One Sunday, my father was out sweeping the long driveway. Lucy was keeping him company as he worked. When the job was done, the two walked together back to the house. Lucy trotted ahead straight toward the flower bed. My father, broom in hand, decided to chase her out of the flower bed. It's important to note that he did NOT hit her with the broom handle. He swished her with the brush-side of the broom. You could tell Lucy didn't like that. She cried out with a horrifying squeal so loud it made my father jump slightly backwards. Suddenly Lucy realized she was in pursuit and the game was on. My father ran for the house with the squealing pig behind him. The next day, she waited in the bushes for his car to arrive. As soon as he stepped from the car, she let out her squeal and the chase was on. This chase went on for the remainder of Lucy's life. She never chased anyone else. Carlene failed to acknowledge this as a problem. In fact, not once did Lucy chase my father if Carlene was in sight. She knew better. Carlene explained to my father, that if he couldn't out run a 500 pound pig that was *his* problem. We all knew Lucy meant no harm, she just enjoyed the thrill of the chase. I will never forget the sight of my father running to the house, in a suit with his doctor's bag in hand, at his heels was Lucy, squealing away.

All the while my father was being chased daily by the pet pig, the children of the farm were being chased by the pet rooster. Our farm was the neighborhood farm in the 1970's. The farm attracted kids from all over town who enjoyed spending days hanging out with the array of animals. It was in the day when no one worried about lawsuits. Kids fell off ponies, rode bareback, and did the heavy lifting on the farm. The rooster was Carlene's way of weeding out the weak. He never had a name. He was just "The Rooster". He was a beautiful creature. The Rooster would strut proudly around the farm and crow defiantly (and often). Despite his grace and beauty, he was god-awful mean, ornery and fast. He would chase anyone, at anytime. He would warn of his aggression by strutting in a circle slowly around his victim. He would fluff his wings and puff out his chest. Next, he would drop a wing as he stepped slowly sideways toward you. That was the take-flight moment, and time to sprint towards anything for protection. Having a small chicken-sized brain, he was easily outsmarted. I am not sure whether (like Lucy), he never wanted to catch us, or he was just easily outrun by children and adults of all ages, but he never did catch anyone. After having been chased by the rooster, most children never returned. Those who did return were inducted into the farm. They wanted to be on the farm so badly they were willing to endure being hunted and chased daily. Everyone who passed the rooster test, learned the carefully crafted lessons of Crazy Carlene, lessons that stay with us today as we navigate the complexities of modern life.

The adventures and challenges of farm living are endless and present indispensable life lessons for all. One of my earliest lessons, beyond how to outrun a rooster, was to think outside of the box. There were countless examples of creative thinking over the years. My first recollection was when Linus went missing.

One of the responsibilities for the kids on the farm was to make sure everyone was accounted for and appeared healthy every morning at breakfast and every evening at dinner. When I mean everyone, I include the animals. At any given time we had over 50 animals to account for; horses, dogs, ponies, pigs, donkeys, sheep, llamas, rabbits, cows and of course The Rooster. While it was the responsibility of the kids to account for all the animals, it seemed that it was the responsibility of the animals to get loose and find trouble each night. The animals would get busy after dark testing fences, ensuring that every latch was closed, and digging holes for escape routes. The donkeys were especially good at slithering under the fences. It was amazing to me that a miniature donkey that stood 36 inches high could slither under a fence that was 18 inches high, but they managed to escape constantly. Most of the neighbors were tolerant of the horses stealing pies off the kitchen window sill and had come to expect donkeys grazing on their front lawn. However, they were never pleased to find that Lucy had visited their flower beds.

One day, Linus went missing. Linus was a 14 hand palomino pony who we found tied to the tree at the end of the driveway. He was abandoned by someone who was kind enough to tie a note around his neck that said, "My name is Linus. I am a nice pony. I need a home." That was enough for a lifelong admission to the farm. We had Linus for many years before one morning he vanished. We looked everywhere. We called the neighbors who soon joined the search. The search party grew throughout the day, yet still no sign of Linus. As the afternoon started to turn to evening, we had searched every inch of the farm, the surrounding homes, the woods, and were starting to suspect foul play. Then we heard an odd noise coming from the old pump house.

The pump house was a scary place. It was basically a small shed like structure with a 10 foot circular well inside (actually a cistern). That is where we found Linus, at the bottom of the hole. Somehow, he had pushed open the old door to the well only to step inside and fall to the bottom. There he stood, perfectly healthy, 12 feet down. Carlene rushed in and quickly surveyed the situation. She instructed us to somehow get hay and grain down to poor Linus and then disappeared into the house.

About an hour later people began arriving with pails and buckets. Many people, neighbors, family friends, my father's patients, they had all been instructed to grab a bucket and meet at the farm. No one had any idea their role in pulling Linus from the well. Others started to arrive with prepared foods and beer. Finally the plan came together when a dump truck arrived and dumped a 12-foot high pile of sand next to the well. We began filling pails of sand and pouring the sand carefully into the hole. The crowd formed an assembly line, passing pails of sand and slowly the pony began to rise to the surface. It was late in the night when Linus finally stepped from the well. The community rejoiced. And the well had been permanently filled with sand so there would be no chance for a reoccurrence. Problem solved.

Being on a farm was physically hard work. Having more than plenty to do, the children on the farm never struggled with weight issues. We were all healthy, strong and physically fit kids who rarely fought with each other. There was little complaining and no blaming. We worked together in harmony. We learned that hard work can be fun and that accomplishments (like pulling a pony from the well) can be emotionally rewarding. That was until the circus came to town...

2. THE CIRCUS

There was plenty of work on the farm to keep a small army of children busy. Size was no concern. The smallest children were assigned the job of 'ON/OFF' where they would man the spigot attached to a hose. Older kids would go from stall to stall filling water buckets shouting "ON" for the "ON/OFF" kid to turn the water on and "OFF" when the bucket was full. I remember being promoted from "ON/OFF" to the other end of the hose, it was a defining moment of accomplishment for me.

Kids on the farm were not allowed to sleep-in. The routine of feeding animals was scheduled to begin at 7 a.m. sharp. It began with the ceremony of raising the flag in the front yard. All the children would arrive and assemble. Carlene would emerge from the house carrying the folded flag at exactly 7 a.m. We would carefully unfold the flag, raise it to full mast briskly, and say the pledge of allegiance before we went off to our daily chores. Thinking back, it seems rather odd that we raised the flag each morning. But this morning ceremony instilled routine, respect and discipline - and we all learned to get up early and to be on time.

During the summers, the number of children grew. One night in June, Carlene took us all to see the Ringling Brother's Circus. As the 12 children sat quietly mesmerized by the flash and glitter of the greatest show on earth, Carlene's mind was buzzing. She had landed on a new idea of how to harness the power of this small army of children to benefit humanity. She decided the children would put together a circus using the animals on the farm by August. We would charge admissions and all proceeds would go to charity.

On the way home she unveiled her plan. No one balked at the challenge. We all got busy the next day planning and training the horses, ponies, donkeys, sheep and Lucy. Carlene built a circular ring and the other mothers in town gathered to sew clown suits. It came together quickly. A circus was born, and was well attended that August afternoon. The proceeds from our first circus raised $900 for Project Hope, a medical ship that delivered care to towns in Africa.

Then over the next 5 years, the circus grew bigger and better. It began to draw larger crowds (over 1000). We built a maze of hay bales in the hayloft and a slide for kids to slide from the hayloft to the barnyard. More importantly, we learned priceless lessons. We learned how to operate as a team. We learned that success was short-lived and failure was imminent. We learned how to anticipate disasters, mitigate risks, accept failures and most importantly that blame was irrelevant since Carlene held us ALL accountable for failures. Fighting and arguing was simply not allowed. By positioning herself often as the enemy she taught us to be allies explaining that "Allies are people with a common enemy." Carlene was the Alpha in the herd. We all loved, feared and respected her.

Circus Practice, 1974

Our failures were mostly benign. Despite endless training, practice and rehearsals, we were no Ringling Brothers. Ponies, puppies, and donkeys trained by children were unpredictable. As the audiences grew, stage fright became an issue for both the children and animals. Our carefully choreographed acts often became jumbled and controlled chaos. We would forget our routines, or the animals would become distracted by the crowd. For example, Lucy would prefer to sniff through the purses in the front row for treats rather than do her tricks.

There were unintended consequences of bad decisions. Silk clown suits seemed a good idea until we discovered the slippery fabric makes it impossible to stay aboard clean shiny ponies. We learned this lesson when all three child circus performers fell off their ponies in the ring. When the three ponies trotted back to the barn and the fallen clowns took a bow the crowd seemed to think it was just part of the show. It was entertainment in its purest form.

The most memorable moment of the circus for me was the monkey. My father had a patient who owned a monkey. Not a small apartment size monkey, but an ape sized monkey. The monkey was aged, and as a result had become periodically insane. He was a loving monkey to his owner for 20 years. But in his old age he had grown aggressive and had on several occasions attacked his owner inflicting lacerations that my father subsequently stitched. On the afternoon before the circus, my father put 27 stitches in the owner's knee. The owner explained that he planned to euthanize the monkey on Monday because as he explained it, "his time had come." My father jumped at the opportunity, and asked if we could borrow the monkey for the weekend. Somehow the deal was arranged and the monkey arrived within hours. He was aggressive only towards men so Carlene carefully held his hand and walked him to a stall in the barn as all of the men hid from sight. The monkey had a small leather collar and was chained to the wall. The chain would allow him to come within 5 feet of the door but not close enough to reach onlookers if the door was open. We were all very excited to have the monkey for the circus. We had no idea of his fate on Monday.

The next morning, I woke with great anticipation. I was so excited I dashed out to the barn with my sister Gwen and stepsister Priscilla. We went straight to the monkey stall and opened the door to get a full view. Well, the monkey obviously was a having a moment of insane aggression just as the stall door opened. He lunged through the air at us with his teeth snarling. Yikes! We fell backwards, scrambling, screaming as we realized his small leather collar had snapped off. Our flight & retreat instincts were well rehearsed after years of running from the Rooster. We spun in unison, and dashed in a methodical pursuit to the house 100 yards away. The monkey was close behind. I remember looking back as the monkey swung along the white fence leading to the house.

Fortunately, we made it to the house that was full of young children changing into clown costumes. The circus goers were to begin arriving in an hour. My parents were fairly calm as they discussed the options. My father had a gun between the mattress and box spring, and kept a single bullet in his underwear drawer. Carlene wanted to try a less dramatic solution first. She went outside with a banana in one hand and a dog leash in the other. We all watched from the window as the monkey approached slowly for the banana. She slipped the leash over his head. The monkey simple reached up and took off the leash. Carlene slipped it on again. The monkey took it off again.

The children were piled six deep watching from the window. My father was at the front door with a gun in hand loaded with the single bullet. The monkey had finished the banana and was still unleashed. Nervously, Carlene pulled a second banana from her pocket and tried to hold the monkey's hand. The monkey took the banana but not her hand. The monkey grew agitated. He snarled and began to bounce around Carlene. My father panicked and fired the single shot at the monkey. It was an awful sight. The monkey fell over. Carlene grabbed a plastic trash can and quickly placed it over the monkey. It was a dramatic moment in the house. The children were horrified. My parents explained the danger of the loose monkey. We all tried to rally as a team, because "the show must go on."

We finished suiting-up in our clown suits, applying white make up and headed toward the door. In a shocking moment that I will never forget, we opened the door to see the monkey standing next to the plastic trash can, fully alive and snarling, obliviously really mad now. We all scrambled back in the house. The house erupted in search of another bullet. We dug through father's underwear drawer, then the sock drawer. There were no more bullets. He began calling friends asking to borrow bullets (I guess there was an unspoken agreement that the bullets would not be returned). Surprisingly, he was able to find someone who had bullets. He went through the garage, jumped safely into his car and drove off in pursuit of bullets. It seemed like hours, but in reality, it was only minutes before he returned. He rolled down the window in his Lincoln Continental and began firing off a round of bullets. It was like a scene from the Godfather. Hours later, the show went on and that night we laid the monkey to rest in a small ceremony including crying children, flowers and a makeshift gravestone.

3. CONSEQUENCES

We were faced with many emergencies growing up on the farm. It is interesting to reflect on what was and was not considered an emergency. In 1970, a horse stuck in a well was not an emergency, rather a community concern. If that were to happen today it would make nightly news. Shooting a monkey in the front yard would be broadcast nationwide.

Growing up on a farm is dangerous and accidents do happen. Sometimes I look back and wonder how we all survived. There were twenty children, twenty ponies, and a barnyard filled with danger. There were no warning labels and Darwinism was in full effect. Common sense was expected. Farm kids are raised with consequences that reach far beyond the wrath of a scolding parent. On a farm (as in life), there are so many unanticipated and random hardships, it is best to calculate risks carefully and never carelessly tempt fate.

My first lesson on the farm was of electricity. Carlene left me near Mable's (the cow) pasture when I was three years old. She said, "don't touch that electric fence." A curious toddler, I needed to know what would happen if I touched the electric fence. I grabbed hold of the fence with my full hand and learned that bad things happened when I disobey. In that instance, I learned to do as I was told and from that point forward there was never any yelling, punishing or spanking. I was always told what was expected of me and I did as I was told. Later as a teenager, I certainly thought long and hard about consequences (and the likelihood of getting caught) before I pursued any trouble.

Another lesson was learned when I tied my pony (Tinker) to a wheelbarrow. It was lunch time. I was eight years old and hungry. There was a wheelbarrow by the front door. It seemed like a perfect plan at the time. I tied Tinker to the wheelbarrow and went into the house to grab something edible from the fridge. I would only be gone for a few seconds....

Tinker immediately put her head down to eat grass and seemed content. I watched closely from the kitchen window. She was fine until she moved toward better grass and the reins pulled the wheelbarrow to follow her. I saw her head jolt up in fear. Horses are flight animals and lack human intelligence. Tinker was not afraid of wheelbarrows, but this particular wheelbarrow seemed to be chasing her. That was all it took, the flight instinct prevailed and off she went, galloping around the property, then down the long driveway toward the road. As she frantically galloped, the wheelbarrow was dragged along by the reins and bouncing on its

Tinkerbell 1973

side near the pony's hind legs. Tinker was terrified. Just as she neared the end of the driveway and onto the busy street, the reins broke and she was freed from the evil wheelbarrow. I sprinted across the big field to Tinker who stood slightly bloodied and shaking. She had cuts and scrapes from the metal wheelbarrow, but was ultimately fine. I was shaking harder than poor Tinker. It was so amazing to me how quickly the pony went from eating contently to near death, while I was absolutely powerless to save her from the on-coming cars. On that day I began to grasp the relationship between a bad decision, an instant in time, and unintended consequences.

When I was 10, it seemed like a good idea to climb on the chicken coop roof. The roof was 12 feet high. The risks of injury were slight. If I were to fall, the inside of the chicken coop offered a soft landing of piles of hay used for nesting chickens. The roof appeared somewhat tattered but I assumed it would hold my weight. I assumed wrong, and fell right through the roof onto a water trough and broke my arm. I learned it is dangerous to make assumptions. Despite calculating risks, there may still be an unanticipated hard landing.

Another notable bad decision was when I was in my teens. I decided it was a good idea to drink alcohol with a group of friends in the cabin on the farm. Actually, the teens were not my friends. I thought if they saw how cool I was, they would all scramble to be my friend. Being able to get alcohol and drink alcohol would definitely make me cool and friend-worthy.

My plan failed on many different levels. I poured a little bit of alcohol from each bottle in my parent's liquor cabinet into a big glass jar. The four teens then drank the entire jar. An hour later we were staggering around the front lawn of the cabin. I don't remember much else from that evening. I do remember it was 7:01 a.m. when Carlene appeared at the door. She seemed unfazed by the condition of the four teenagers or the cabin. It was time to feed the animals and get to work. She had planned a work day for me. My job was to move hay from one side of the loft to the other. I had never consumed alcohol before and therefore had never had the pleasure of a hangover. I experienced the full extent of my first hangover in the sweltering August heat in the hay loft. I still felt a little drunk, definitely nauseated, and was surprised my head didn't explode. It was a new level of 'just awful' for me. By the way, there was no reason to move the hay in the loft other than to teach me the perils of alcohol consumption, which it did. I have been a lifelong moderate drinker.

4. NEW KID IN TOWN

Carlene, 1976

The small town of Lynnfield, Massachusetts began to grow in around our little farm. Soon the town's people were not so pleased when our herd of 20 donkeys got loose and ran down Main Street. Next, our four farm dogs were expected to be on a leash at all times. The police complained when we tied our ponies to the pillar in front of the bakery when we rode to town for an afternoon éclair. My parents finally decided it was time to move onward. We have all heard the saying "When you are getting run out of town, get out in front and make it look like a parade." Well, I have personally lived that saying. The circus paraded through town, the animals were loaded and off we went to new adventures.

I was 14 that summer when "Crazy Acres" moved to Ipswich, Massachusetts. I was anxious to meet new friends and very self conscious as teenage girls are. I was tall, thin and gangly. Starting school was difficult for me. The other girls seemed so "country girl polished" to me. I was different. I had horses to feed and farm chores to do. To make matters worse, the house was not finished when we arrived so my parents rented a camper and I lived in the dressing room of our gooseneck horse trailer until late September. Fitting in was further complicated by the eccentric Carlene.

I was at the age when kids are slightly embarrassed that they actually have parents. And to be honest, I had a lot to be embarrassed about. Carlene had adopted her own version of Fashionista. Her wardrobe was the intersection of practicality and fashion. Every fall she would go to Sears and buy 7 pairs of jeans and 7 turtlenecks. That was her winter fashion. When the warm spring weather arrived, she would simply cut off the legs of the jeans, and the arms and neck off the turtlenecks, and that was her summer fashion wear which often included a bandana tied around her head to hold her long hair back. Cowboy boots were comfortable year round.

In Massachusetts, young adults are eligible to get their drivers permit at age 16. This allows them to drive a car during the daylight hours with a licensed driver in the passenger seat. Young adults then can get their full driver's license at age 16 and-a-half. By the time I turned 16, Carlene was tired of driving me around. So instead of getting a permit to drive a car, I got my permit to drive a motorcycle. I was given a barely road-worthy old motorcycle, a Honda 250cc. A motorcycle permit allows motorcyclists to drive themselves during daylight hours, but restricts them from taking passengers or driving after dark. This was a perfect solution for Carlene, as it would relieve her from the responsibility of driving me to school each day. The only problem was I turned 16 in January. To solve this problem, Carlene went to the local Salvation Army store and bought a Men's large blue polyester snowmobile suit for me. Some of the kids in school actually thought it was cool that I drove to school in January on a motorcycle, others - well, not-so-much.

I never had a date to my junior or senior prom. I was shy and awkward around boys. I was different than the average teenager, and during high school being different was not socially acceptable. It took me many years to accept and embrace being different.

5. ANIMAL EPISODES

"We supply animals for movies, commercials and special promotions."

The business idea for Animal Episodes came was Carlene was asked to join the 'Committee to Establish a Veterinary School in New England'. The committee wanted to make a television commercial, and the estimated expense for the filming was astronomical. They found the reason it was so high was the video company had made provision for the cost of renting trained animals from an agency in New York. There sat Carlene with a bunch of extremely well socialized animals trained by a rag-tag bunch of neighborhood kids for the summer circus. So she offered to provide all the animals for the first commercial for Tuft's. The animals played their part perfectly and Tuft's saved thousands of dollars. Suddenly, Carlene's name started to be passed around the media community as a source of animals. Having proved she was willing and capable of handling most animals, Animal Episodes became New England's provider of animals for movies, TV and print ads.

While Animal Episodes came into being by filling a need for the Tufts commercial, there also was a great deal of thought on "How can I make these farm yard pets tax deductable?" While most people start a business with careful market analysis, needs assessment, or perhaps even write a business plan - well, not Crazy Carlene. She had no time for that – she had a business to run!

We had accumulated quite a herd of miniature donkeys. It all began with one male donkey "Don Quixote" (of La Mancha). We nicknamed him "Donkey". Donkey seemed lonely so we adopted him several lady friends to keep him company. Nature took its course and soon we had a herd of 20. There was a very small market for miniature donkeys and Donkey's production far exceeded demand. Each donkey was hand raised and part of the family. We couldn't bear to part with any of them, yet we were challenged to figure out what to do with all the donkeys. As usual, it didn't take long for Carlene to create a work plan.

Her new plan was to teach the eight donkeys to pull a carriage. Each donkey in the collection was under 32 inches high. The Great Danes were bigger. Since we had no equipment to fit their petite size, Carlene ordered an $8,500 harness from Sam Freeman. He made a similar harness for the Budweiser Clydesdales. Next, she ordered a custom carriage from the same maker of the carts for the Queen of England. When the custom carriage was finished, she drove to Reading, Pennsylvania to pick it up and came home with the carriage plus three miniature bulls, one cow and a full size caboose. It was never good when Carlene went on a road trip. She would come home with all sorts of things.

Our donkeys were dressed in the finest harness, pulling a sparkling new miniaturized custom cart. The only problem was they were completely untrained. They were friendly and would follow you around but many were not even halter-broken. These donkeys were backyard pets - loving, cuddly little creatures that loved to be patted, scratched, and fed treats. They had never worked a day in their lives.

Carlene chose the path of least resistance. She trained only the two lead donkeys to drive. They marched around the yard until the two male donkeys could steer and stop on command. It didn't take long because donkeys are very smart. The problem was that all miniature donkeys look exactly the same: grey with a dorsal stripe. Finding the two trained donkeys in the herd of look-alikes was often challenging. Fortunately, you knew immediately when you had the wrong donkey in the leading spot. To avoid future mishap, Carlene gave the two lead donkeys a unique haircut so they were easy to spot in the herd – which I am sure caused them to be ridiculed by their donkey friends.

Days before their first paying-gig, we hitched the team for the first time. The poor donkeys seemed slightly confused as we hooked them all together. One young donkey just lay down. He wanted no part of the hitch until he learned that the whole team was powered by carrots, a fact that served as a morale booster for all eight donkeys. The team of donkeys moved off slowly. The front two donkeys were actually pulling the other six. Carlene had recruited several teenagers to feed carrots along the way. It was an exhausting morning of accomplishment, but the team was now officially ready for business. And so a hitch was born and paraded through the streets of Boston the following day in front of thousands of people.

The donkey hitch went on parading around New England. It would take 40 minutes to harness them up. Because of their size, it was backbreaking labor. I think the donkeys even started to enjoy the carrots and attention from the crowd. From the donkeys' standpoint, they probably also concluded the only safe place was in the middle of the road, rather than among the cheering crowd lining the route.

With so much visibility in Boston, the Animal Episode phone started to ring. One call was to bring a few donkeys to a fundraising event for the Democratic Party. It seemed simple enough. We marched six donkeys through the elaborate hotel lobby and onto the elevator. The party was a dashing and well attended gala: a black tie and with an overflowing scrumptious buffet. It was too crowded to have the donkeys on lead ropes. After a few embarrassing entanglements with expensive gowns, we decided it was easiest to just let the donkeys loose to mingle. Of course, the donkeys immediately mingled their way right up to the buffet. Being so small we were worried we would lose sight of them so we tied helium balloons to their halters. My only job for the evening was to stand by the buffet and make sure the donkeys didn't help themselves. We could see the movement of the balloons through the party guests as we ate raw oysters and lobster tails.

One important note is that donkeys are very neat with their 'potty times' and don't like to relieve themselves inside buildings. They seem to know to relieve themselves in the trailer so it is fairly safe to let them wander, although we always kept an eye on them – or more specifically, on their tails. One of my revered skills is that I can spot a donkey-pooper-in-the-works and have been known to leap and bound across a crowd to make '*the save*' with utmost grace. I am the best pooper scooper that ever lived – fast & efficient. My skills also include being able to catch a swan without out injury and to catch a flying pigeon with one hand. I was trained young that every job that is worth doing is worth doing well no matter how big or how small. No job was beneath my pay grade.

Animal Episodes did the traditional "petting zoo", but never booked small jobs. We would only book big venues, larger hotels and fundraisers, never a 'Suzie's-fifth-birthday-party' type job. The bookings paid well which kept the farm deductable and surprisingly profitable for the first time ever. In addition, the animals seemed to love the attention. It appeared to be a win-win for everyone involved. I had graduated college and decided to pursue a graduate degree at Boston University. Therefore, I was always interested in earning money to offset tuition bills. I jumped at chance to earn $10 an hour as did many of my classmates. As a result, we had some premier talent manning the zoo.

Carlene was particularly handy at building things so she built a modular portable barnyard neatly painted red with a stall for every animal. It assembled in 15 minutes. The animals hung out in their portable stalls and came to the edge when they wanted to be fed, which for the donkeys was *always*.

One of the premier attractions was the baby-chickens. I assume that not many people know that you can order baby chickens through the mail. I had no idea either until the FedEx truck arrived with a package chirping away. We were equally surprised to find

100 baby chickens inside the box. The driver mumbled, "well that's a first" as he drove away. The baby chickens were ALL alive. Baby chickens are amazingly resilient. I carried the box to Carlene's office, unfazed as always, she explained that they were for the next day's job.

The following day we set up our unusual petting zoo with the portable barnyard. Typically, there is not much to do when manning the petting zoo other than people watch. We would have to watch that the spectators did not feed their own fingers to our animals. We supplied paddles and a small Dixie cup of grain for the public to feed the animals. Undoubtedly, there was always some teenager who would try feeding the animals something they shouldn't be eating – like a hotdog, napkin or their own finger. Donkeys don't like to eat fingers. It was always fun to hear 'city folk' try to explain to children the simple facts about barnyard animals. Many times they thought the donkeys were baby horses. We'd hear all the bacon jokes as they passed Lucy the pig sleeping peacefully in her bed of straw.

Petting zoos were a cash cow for me and for my graduate student friends. We'd bring textbooks and often sit in the straw along with Lucy studying as the on lookers passed by. It was the perfect gig until the chick table was introduced. Then it was all-hands-on-deck to manage the chaos. Small children would stand six deep around the table mesmerized at the sight of the fluffy yellow chicks. Our job was to help the children gently pick up a chick and watch closely as they carefully held the chick. We tried to encourage parents to help. Most parents were standoffish while most children couldn't contain their excitement, which left the person manning the chicken table in the precarious position of trying to keep order in chaos and often yelling at other people's kids. The majority of the children were perfect angels; it was the others that created the problem. Kids would try to grab a chick

behind your back, try to see how many chicks they could stack in one hand, or get scared and drop the chick on the grass amongst the swarm of children. We even had one adult who stuffed her pockets with the baby chickens and tried to sneak off. Fortunately, her chirping pockets gave her away.

Watching the chick table was far more exhausting for us than for the chicks. We would only put 20 on the table at a time, and rotate the little guys frequently. It was made clear to all of us that if we didn't leave with 100 LIVE chicks, we would ALL be held accountable. We were all very nervous every time we counted and loaded the chicks at the end of the day. We were never made accountable because we never lost a chick.

The city of Boston called us to ask if we would bring the petting zoo to the Boston Common for the entire month of December as part of a festive Christmas celebration. They agreed to build a semi-permanent enclosure for a small group of animals and provide a night watchman. On the last weekend we were to provide two live reindeers for the final celebration on the State House steps. It seemed like a good idea at the time and the contract was signed.

For almost four weeks everything went according to plan. The animals were loving the job. They were in their element – food and attention, what else could they ask for? All seemed too perfect. Then on the last weekend things went horribly wrong. The baby donkey that appeared to be sleeping all day didn't get up for dinner. She was actually dead. She had been running around and playful in the morning then apparently lay down for an afternoon nap and died. This put us into a tailspin. She was six months old and healthy (we would later do an autopsy and find that the poor thing was born with a congenital heart defect. It was a miracle she even survived six months). But the poor donkey baby died and we needed to get her to the vet for an autopsy. We had no means to smuggle her off the Boston Common unnoticed. We told onlookers she was sleeping. In a panic, I ran for my car and parked it behind the tent. I grabbed the baby donkey and put her peacefully in my arms walked purposefully through the crowd, out the back, and put her in the trunk of my car. Crisis averted, and by 5 p.m. we were on schedule to bring the reindeer up to the State House for the début with Santa and the Governor of Massachusetts.

State officials had constructed a small paddock enclosure to house the reindeer during the ceremony. The reindeer were borrowed from a farm in Vermont. They arrived with one handler. I was relieved to find they were fairly friendly and well trained. However, I took one look at the enclosed paddock and wondered if the building planners had considered that it is rumored that reindeer can fly. It seemed short, not overwhelmingly short, but definitely short. Maybe I have seen the Rudolf movie too many times, but I would have built it six feet tall rather than four. The reindeers' handler did not seem to even notice the height and immediately unleashed them.

Both reindeer stood there rather peacefully for a several minutes nibbling on the hay provided and watching the growing crowd. When the TV camera and crew started to arrive, the reindeer stopped eating and began to resemble "two deer in the headlights". More people, more equipment, the Governor and Santa all arrived. Yet, it was the moment they switched on the glaring spotlight that the reindeer literally took flight. I learned the truth. Reindeer really do fly. They were completely loose on the State House lawn. They darted in and out of the crowd. I was sure that their full-set of antlers were going to take someone's eye out, or worse. I got my chance as the smaller of the two barreled towards the steps to Beacon Street. I leapt through the air like I had seen the cowboys do on TV. I grabbed an antler pulling his head sideways and was able to wrestle him to the ground. I held tight while others arrived with a lead and halter. The second reindeer suddenly stopped. He knew the thrill was over and let the handler attach a lead to his halter.

As I climbed to my feet, I noted my knees were shaking from the excitement. I saw that both reindeer were fine and unscathed. I gasped when I noticed in my hand was an antler that had broken off during the scuffle. How terrible. How embarrassing. I broke the reindeer. Despite the mishap and the one antlered reindeer, the show went on. This time the handler stayed in the news clip holding both reindeers' lead tightly. On the walk down to the tent, the handler explained that reindeer antler shed frequently. I still felt badly, so badly I completely forgot about the donkey in my trunk for several days. It was winter and by the time I dropped off the donkey for an autopsy the body had frozen. The receptionist at the vet clinic stared blankly at me as I tried to explain that donkey had not died from hypothermia. I went on to say I had completely forgotten the body in my trunk. Based on her expression, I could tell she was thinking "What responsible pet owner forgets about a dead animal in a trunk?" I didn't have a good answer, so I quickly turned and left the waiting room. Sometimes it is important to know when it is time to say nothing.

6. COMMERCIALS & MOVIES

Boston was full of opportunity for the film makers and photographers who began to contact Animal Episodes for animal actors and models. There were simple requests like a dog sleeping at someone's feet, or more complicated requests like a dog biting the rear of a postman. We supplied parrots, pigs, frogs, cats, lizards, swans, shampooed cows and more: any domestic animal. For wildlife, like lions, tigers and bears, we would subcontract with an animal agency in New York City.

Animal Episodes was the perfect match for Carlene's ingenious mind. Every shot required a masterful combination of treats and trickery to get the animal to act as the producer or photographer expected.

Question: How do you prevent domestic ducks from flying away during an outdoor filming?

Answer: Use fishing lines tied gently around their delicate feet.

Question: How do you get a horse to talk like Mr. Ed?

Answer: With a small amount of peanut butter beneath their upper lip.

Question: How do you get a mouse to stand still under the lights in a studio?

Answer: Place a large strainer over the mouse and a small morsel of cheese in front of the mouse. Remove strainer slowly. Take photos quickly.

Question: How do you get four pigs dressed in harness with antlers to stand still for six seconds at Christmas time?

Answer: Place pigs on a three foot high platform. Four people squat below the platform with spray bottles filled with water mixed with honey. In unison, spray the honey mix into the four pigs mouths for ten seconds. Everyone duck down quickly for 6 seconds. Take photos quickly. Of course the only problem with that tactic was everything sticks to honey, especially fake snow - something the average person would not know, unless they had to provide four pigs in harness attached to a sleigh for a winter wonderland photo shoot with fake snow. I felt as if I had been 'tarred & feathered' by the end of the day.

I had finished my first graduate degree and decided to continue on for a Ph.D. Basically, I decided to be a starving graduate student and indentured employee to Animal Episodes for an indefinite period of time. While other graduate students were waiting tables and interning, I was busy as a pig wrangler, cat handler, donkey chaser, horse jockey, stagecoach driver, and swan transporter. It was never boring.

Carlene would often send me off to do small jobs on my own. When I arrived on the farm, she would hand me a colored index card with instructions scribbled on one side and an address on the other, usually some studio in Boston. The instructions were always slightly vague. I would load up animals, crates of animals and boxes of any equipment needed. We had standard kits for each animal. For example, our 'dog kit' included dog treats, leashes, collars, brushes, and toys. Our 'cat kit' included cat food, band aids, antiseptic ointment, safety glasses and thick gloves. I always hated cat jobs, especially when we would use our not-so-friendly, partially feral, barn cats that we rescued from the local shelter. I am not sure why, but all cats just don't like me. I would end up getting bitten and scratched by the end of the day even when we borrowed a nice house cat from friends. If there is a way to put a cat in a crate without being bitten and scratched, I never figured it out.

We never would use drugs to control the animal or harm any animal in any way. Animal jobs were diverse. The animals were borrowed from different sources and always returned safely. We handled the swans that swam in Boston's public gardens. Each fall, I would have to wrangle the swans without out injury (to the swan or myself) and bring them home for the winter only to return them to the commons in the spring. Beautiful creatures, but swans are defensive birds and don't like to be caught or handled in any way. Not being an experienced swan handler, I worried about being bitten. On my first attempt I focused on the swan's beak. He must have known I was a rooky at swan management. He spun quickly and grabbed hold of my forearm before I even knew what happened. In that instant I was relieved to learn that swans have no teeth. Then not so pleased to learn it's not the teeth you need to worry about; it's the wings that do the damage. The swan grabbed hold of my arm with its beak only to pummel me with his wings. I looked like a victim of domestic abuse the next day. But I am a quick study when it comes to managing animals. I only got pummeled once before I learned the proper way to catch a swan.

Looking back, I wish Google had existed back then so I could have Googled "How to catch a swan" before making the attempt.

We supplied a horse for Paul Revere to ride through Boston for one of the first cellular telephones ads. The phone was the size of a brief case. The horse wasn't pleased about the large briefcase hanging from his side, but he marched proudly in front of the camera. Not all jobs went that well.

One less successful job was for a movie with Goldie Hawn. The call was for brown ducks. We rounded up several ducks from a local farmer's yard and took them to Plymouth, Massachusetts. We sat all day under the actors' tent eating well and waiting patiently to film the ducks. Finally, at 4:30 p.m. the director called for the ducks to be placed in the pond. Carlene and I boarded a small row boat with a basket of ducks and I rowed out into the middle of the pond. The plan was to place the ducks, row away for the shot, and return with a net to catch the ducks after the 20 second shot had been captured on film. I pulled the first two ducks from the basket and handed them to Carlene who gently placed them in the water. Then I handed her the next two. As she placed the second group in the water, we heard someone scream from the shoreline. "The ducks are sinking!" And they were sinking, actually drowning. The ducks had disappeared under the surface. I quickly jumped from the boat as several people from shore had also begun to frantically wade out. The water was shallow and clear so it was easy to grab the ducks under the water. I grabbed two and members of the crew grabbed the other two.

It turns out that not all ducks swim! We learned that ducks need to preen their feathers before they are able to float (something a simple Google search would of advised us of had Google been an around back in the early 90's). Since this particular group of ducks had never preened their feathers, they sunk. We returned the next day with a new set of ducks that had first been tested in the bathtub. The ducks swam on cue.

Some days I would be driving into Boston with a cooler full of butterflies, a shoe box of Praying Mantis, or box of cockroaches. Other days, I would have snakes, lizards or a small cow. Pigeons were popular in many movies. One famous movie "Blown Away", was filmed in Boston. We supplied pigeons for scenes throughout that movie. Whenever I see a pigeon in a movie, I am always reminded of having a shirt full of pigeons and tossing them in front of the camera. Jobs with homing pigeons fascinated me. The pigeons would fly home and be waiting for me when I pulled in the driveway. Per the Animal Rights Laws, only banded homing pigeons could be used in films.

On one particular morning I was instructed to meet at the farm at 6 a.m. I arrived, slightly groggy but on time. My father was standing by the pickup truck looking curiously at the instructions on the colored index card. He and I were going to do a "Rabbit Job" together. He had rescheduled his day of patients and was taking this time to go on an adventure with me. We climbed in the pickup truck where between us sat a stack of laundry baskets. My first question was "Where do we pick up the Rabbits?" He calmly `said, "They're in the back of the truck." I spun in my seat and peered out the back window of the truck to find the entire bed of the truck was filled with a sea of rabbits. There must have been 100 gigantic, fluffy white

rabbits back there. Fortunately the truck had a cap on covering the cab. My next question was, "What are the laundry baskets for?" He smiled and answered, "To move the rabbits." My final question, "Can we stop for coffee? I need more caffeine." And off we drove to a photography studio in downtown Boston.

We arrived and met with the photographer. He explained the ad was for American Express. They wanted to show how customers' savings would multiply "like rabbits" if they signed up for some AMEX reward program. We went back to the truck and loaded two rabbits carefully into each laundry basket. Carrying the baskets, we walked across the street, into the formal lobby, up the elevator, down a long hallway, through double doors and into the studio. We deposited the four rabbits and walked back to the truck. Only 96 more rabbits to go! By the time we got to the final basket loads of rabbits we had the rabbits piled eight high as we scurried across the busy street with rabbit ears bouncing in full view. These rabbits were BIG rabbits. The rabbits seemed entirely content to be stacked in the laundry basket, but the basket was HEAVY. They were so heavy that my dad stumbled on the lobby step and fell on his knees spilling the rabbits. The rabbits were unscathed and darted off in all directions. They were amazingly fast for their size. I couldn't put my basket down or those bunnies would jump out too, so I left my father and the receptionist in the marble lobby chasing rabbits while I delivered my basketful. I returned to find my father holding one rabbit, the receptionist holding another, and a lobby filled with men in business suits chasing rabbits.

After a long day chasing rabbits, we got the shot AMEX wanted. We loaded up all of the rabbits and got them home safely. My father returned to his job as Dr. Thomas White, MD and never offered to go on another Animal Episodes job again. He decided it was easier to save lives than to chase rabbits.

Horses were a frequent request. Boston is always a good site for documentaries and movies seeking to recreate Colonial times. The first movie we did required several horses to pull carriages through historic Beacon Hill. We were asked to supply four horse drawn carriages and drivers. I had only driven donkeys, never horses, but I guess that qualified me as a driver. Finally my big debut in film and the costume designer dressed me as a man! I was quite nervous; the carriage was filled with famous actresses dressed for the part. Carlene shouted to me as I pulled away from the curb and headed toward the State House, "Don't forget the Carriage is NOT a Cut-Under."

I had no idea what a Cut-Under cart was but learned quickly when I went to make a sharp left turn in the narrow streets of Beacon Hill. Cut-Under carriages are designed with the wheels placed underneath the carriage to enable them to make sharp turns. Carriages that are NOT Cut-Under are designed with wheels flush to the carriage. This means on sharp turns the wheels slam into the carriage.

This was a problem. I was following two other carriages that were Cut-Under carriages. I could not make the same sharp turn. I was nervous driving a horse already and this certainly was not helping. I turned the horse back onto Beacon Street, and straight into one-way, on-coming traffic. I didn't know what to do so I just stopped the horse in the intersection.

The traffic was not pleased with the inconvenience of a horse and carriage blocking the flow of traffic in all directions. The loud horns and shouting drivers made the horse anxious. The only thing I could think to do was to go backwards. I pulled on the reins, called the horse's name and shouted, "Back Lincoln." Lincoln must have known we were in trouble, his ears turned quickly toward the carriage. I could tell he was listening to me through the noisy traffic. Lincoln was looking for direction from me and seemed pleased to hear, "Back Lincoln, Back!" He went slowly backwards, then to the side, then backwards again. Instead of an elegant three-point-turn, I carefully choreographed a twelve-point-turn and was on my way. I just kept thinking of the story that might have made the local news if I had failed "Novice driver, tips horse carriage filled with actresses in downtown Boston." Fortunately, Lincoln, whom I had borrowed for the afternoon, seemed to have the whole thing well under control.

All of the horses we had on the farm were at one time rescued from slaughter. A bit of a motley crew of horses, but they seemed to understand that occasionally they would have to behave themselves well enough to avert disaster and justify their feed bill.

One afternoon we received a call for a horse and rider to gallop across a field. Unbeknownst to me, Carlene had rescued a thoroughbred racehorse from the slaughterhouse two days earlier. I was living in Boston and took the train out to meet Carlene on her way to the field I was to gallop across. She failed to explain to me that the horse had been 5th in his last race at Suffolk Downs Racetrack *last week*. That just didn't come up in the conversation. What did come up was that I was to wear a chicken suit.

We arrived at the shoot. The director hurried over excited to meet us and to get me suited up. He was followed closely by the wardrobe specialist carrying a large yellow chicken suit. She in turn was followed by an intern with a large yellow chicken head, and another intern carrying bright orange feet and fluffy yellow hands. To my relief the chicken suit would disguise my face from the camera.

Carlene unloaded the horse. He was thinking it was race day and was obviously very excited. His eyes were wild as he circled nervously around Carlene. He was already saddled and literally 'rearing to go'. He took one look at me in the chicken suit and suddenly appeared more like a Fire-Breathing-Dragon, snorting and circling wildly. Again by strict policy, we never drugged or tranquilized any animal for any shot EVER. Although the situation recommended it, we don't ever so we had to come up with another plan. Carlene decided it was a good time to reveal to me that the horse was fresh from the track. As anyone who knows anything about racehorses knows, these horses have no brakes. The only way to get them to stop is customarily with a lead pony after they are tired from galloping a full race. Pulling on the reins is futile. The plan was to get me on the horse, get me galloping and Carlene would somehow miraculously get the horse to stop. No problem, the chicken suit was well padded. What could go wrong?

Alrighty-then, up I go on to the horse and off he goes like a racehorse bolting from the starting gate. Immediately I noticed a problem. When I separated my legs to stride the saddle the chicken suit rose so that my head sank into the neck of the suit. The chicken suit head was above my head. That nice little screen patch that allows the person wearing the costume to see was now above my head. I could see nothing. I grabbed for the horse's mane, but found it is impossible to grip the mane while wearing fluffy yellow chicken hands. But I remembered that the open field was enclosed by a fence, and that there were no trees to collide with. I resolved to stay calm as we galloped and prayed that Carlene did in fact have a plan for stopping the horse. I tried to pull the reins but as expected the horse did not slow his pace and we galloped on.

It seemed like hours before I felt the horse start to slow; from a full gallop, to a controlled gallop, to a canter, then a trot, and finally a walk. I jumped to the ground, the chicken suit dropped down, and I suddenly had sight again. The first thing I saw was Carlene standing with the horse whose nose was in a bucket (of grain). Thankfully, that particular plan worked - others, well not-so-much.

I had completely forgotten about the "sheep job" until recently when I was at a dinner party and the dinner conversation turned to a light competition on most embarrassing moments. I won. One of my more embarrassing moments was with a sheep in a Mens room in Boston. How did I find myself in a Mens room with a sheep? Again, it was Carlene's idea....

There was a call for a sheep. The print ad was to portray something about a sheep wearing a wolf's pelt as in a "sheep in wolf's clothing". A local gentleman's farm (owned by a professor at MIT) was happy to lend us a sheep. The owner said the sheep was "not too bad to handle." By the way "not too bad to handle" applied only if compared to handling a grizzly bear. But in comparison to handling a *well behaved sheep*, he was difficult to handle only because of his large size and unruly attitude. When we arrived in Boston, Carlene handed me the rope attached to the slightly annoyed sheep and laughed as the sheep dragged me down the street. Horrified pedestrians jumped from the sidewalk.

Once we discovered that he would follow a bucket of grain anywhere, we were finally able to get the sheep into the studio. The sheep had a long entangled coat and obviously had not been sheered lately. He was a bit smelly and quite dirty, but it was a print ad and a clean sheep was not requested. Arriving with a clean sheep was a monumental task for which the customer would have been charged an extra fee. The request was for "just a sheep".

The photo called for the shot to be taken slightly from the rear. After the first roll of film the photographer stared into the lens for several minutes as the sheep stood quietly under the lights. You could tell something was wrong. Then the photographer awkwardly explained that the sheep's "pendulous testicles" were too dark, dirty and hairy for the shot (obviously before the days of photoshopping). The appendages needed to be lightened and trimmed. I was horrified to hear Carlene agree to work on cleaning up the testicles. "No problem" she said. "We can work on those."

Are you kidding? "WE can work on those?" Why did she automatically assume that I would be in on that task? I am a strong believer that you just can't make all customers happy, and I was perfectly content to leave the studio with the sheep (and his dirty testicles). I was not cleaning testicles to make this photographer happy. I was overruled.

The photographer led us down the hall to the Mens room to do the job. I am not sure why we couldn't use the Ladies room, but it was the Mens room where we spread a tarp and sat down to start snipping. At first Mr. Sheep objected but when he realized we were not inflicting any pain he laid on his back quietly as we clipped and scrubbed. After a few minutes the door opened and a man walked into the Mens room. He was wore polished shoes and a sharp business suit with a colorfully coordinated tie. He took one look at the sheep, at both of us, and headed over to the urinal where he unzipped and attended to his business. Afterward, he washed his hands and left without making eye contact or saying a word. Strange what passes for normal in the big city.

7. NORMAL IS OVERRATED

After years of living as a poor college student struggling to pay rent and tuition, I decided it was best to move home to the farm. There was a cozy cottage that I thought would be a nice break from city life. However, Carlene explained that the cottage was not an option. It was designated for the farm manager. I was to live in the caboose. She had bought the caboose several years prior and had had it completely renovated. It had all the necessities with the exception of a shower. I lived in the tiny caboose for over a year building fires in the wood stove for heat and sprinting to the main house for a daily shower usually wrapped in a towel. It was always somewhat awkward when occasionally I would run into visitors along the way. The Fedex delivery man by this time was well accustomed to the strange occurrences that happened at "Crazy Acres".

I tried to help out around the farm on occasion in exchange for my accommodations. Carlene had purchased two young oxen, a bull and a cow. They were miniature cattle: oddly shaped with normal cow-sized torsos and six inch legs. They stood only 36 inches high but weighed over 700lbs. We soon learned the two oxen were actually bulls, but remarkably the four seemed to coexist rather peacefully. The problem began when their horns started to grow. Growing horns are itchy and to relieve the itch the animals had taken to scratching them on the big trees in the pasture. The bark was being ripped away and we feared without adequate bark the trees would die. I offered to wrap the trees with wire mesh fence to prevent the bulls from stripping the bark. It seemed easy enough.

It was a laborious project that I reserved for a Saturday afternoon. The bulls watched with stern eye as I dragged the wire fence into the pasture. They drew closer and closer as the morning went on. By lunch the three bulls stood within ten feet of me and began pawing occasionally while mooing in a snarling, mean way. They grew increasingly agitated as the day went on. Finally, sensing imminent danger, I tip-toed from the pasture and went to the house. I explained to Carlene that the bulls were mean and attempting to charge me. She walked down to the field with me, opened the gate and walked directly over the bulls. "I don't know what your problem is. These bulls are fine", she explained as her hand gently stroked the biggest of them. She stood by the fence and watched me return to work. The bulls stood peacefully, even pretending to graze lightly.

As soon as she left for the house, the second she was out of sight, the bulls returned with their aggressive behavior. How does she do that? By the time I had finished the tree project I had been charged three times. I learned I could outrun the bulls and jump a three-railed split rail fence in a single bound; again that Rooster chasing training had come in handy.

The three bulls and the cow were not the right fit for the farm. Every other animal had been rescued from some untimely doom. These were expensive, pedigreed miniature cattle. God only knows how much Carlene paid for these mean little guys. They were out to kill someone at their earliest convenience. Seeing the looming liability of the bulls, Carlene somehow managed to arrange a swap: the miniature cattle for a mammoth donkey. I am not sure how this arrangement was coordinated, but I was certainly pleased to see the trailer of little cattle leave the farm, and "Mary-the-Donkey" arrived two days later.

Mary was eight months old, a black mammoth donkey. She had long gangly legs, a gigantic head, and enormous ears. We actually measured her head when she arrived. Her head was two feet long and each ear stretched one foot more. She was a bit shy at first, but soon took her place on the farm as 'Head of Household.' No fence or stall would hold her. She figured out latches, slithered under some fences, climbed over others, and as a result was always on the loose. We finally gave up, and her stall door just remained open at all times. We installed "Mary-proof closets" throughout the farm to keep her from eating what was not hers. I doubt she ever really understood that she was not a human.

It was about that time that I graduated and moved away. I had decided it was time to be normal. I got a job, bought a house, got married and had a baby. Finally, I was normal! Unfortunately, I married a man who became an alcoholic. Nice man, but the alcohol got the best of him. My son was 6 months old when I moved back to the cabin on the farm. I was on my own. It was to be my responsibility to raise my son physically and financially. Life had clipped my wings, but not my spirit. That was the point when I decided it was easier to rescue animals than people.

I was pleased to have better accommodations than the caboose. However, there was a condition attached to living in the cabin, I was not to displace the existing occupant, Rufus. Rufus was another rescue, this time a cockatoo parrot with a bigger-than-life personality for an animal that stood less than a foot tall. He had lived at a private nunnery for many years and had learned to imitate the fire alarms, which had driven even the nuns crazy. Sympathetic to the nuns and the bird, Carlene took Rufus in and put him in the cabin alone at night where no one would be bothered by his frequent (and loud) siren imitations in the middle of the night.

When I moved back to the farm all I had were my clothes, my son and two horses. I told myself it was a blessing to have a place to go, and how bad could it be living with Rufus? Well, Rufus was a character, full of life and had many things to talk about – all the time. Most of the time, he ran around loose in the cabin with us - harmless but noisy. He had things to say, and if we ignored him, he would just say them louder. He would follow me into the bathroom and stand outside the shower just talking random words without any sense. At night he warned us of imaginary fires. At 2 a.m. his fire alarm siren would jolt us out of bed. I would yell down to Rufus to stop. He would just yell right back, repeating my words. Frustrated, I decided on a new strategy. Since he seemed to like to share a bathroom with me while I showered, I inadvertently learned that Rufus didn't like to get wet. I filled a simple spray bottle with water and when he started in with his alarm I sprayed him with a mist of water. Finally silence. It took him only days to connect the fire alarm noise with a mist-spray of water. Problem solved.

I would let Rufus out in the yard every morning for a walk-about. Initially the dogs were curious about the bird and perhaps wanted to eat him. But Rufus was no meal ticket, he chased right after the dogs. They scurried away in fear of the small, but very mean bird. I worried more about the dogs being attacked by Rufus, than Rufus being attacked by the dogs.

Rufus was also a ruthless snake hunter. He would head right off to the garden in search of snakes. Unfortunately, Rufus was not actually hunting snakes, he was hunting our garden hoses. It got to the point where there was not one single working hose on the farm because Rufus had attacked them all. Turning on the hose was

more of an effective irrigation system, than a water source. There were so many holes in every hose it became impossible to fill a bucket.

Rufus was not the only problem I faced living on the farm. There was also Mary-the-Donkey. By now Mary had been influenced by life on the farm. She had developed her own quirky nature. She spent most of her days tagging along after Carlene's golf cart and in constant search of food. Mary was like a giant golden retriever. She would eat anything and was a well documented thief. If you left your car windows or sunroof open she would stretch into your car and grab anything that resembled food, even coffee cups. You could not leave any unattended food on the farm. She had a keen sense of food opportunities and would emerge from the shadows. One time we found her trotting up the driveway with a lunch bag in her mouth, goodness knows where she found that.

Mary loved my son Colby because he was a messy eater and carelessly left food unattended. She would hang unobtrusively over the deck of the cabin looking for a tidbit of Cheerio that may drop from Colby's high chair. She would follow him ever so quietly and carefully hoping he would drop his donut as he wandered on the farm. Mary was very careful not to eat little fingers or step on tiny toes when she would reach out and steal food right out of a child's hand.

I always felt Mary lurking. She knew that my son and I had food. She wanted that food. She could only play cute little hungry donkey for so long. Frustrated, she stepped up her game and eventually figured out how to open the front door of the cabin to graciously let herself in. It was a disaster. She went straight to the kitchen, pulling Cheerio boxes, bags of sugar and noodles from the kitchen shelf. She had quite a feast. The mess took days to clean up. I was furious with Mary. So furious, I rigged up an electric wire around the door handle so Mary would not help herself again. Like me, she knew not to go near wire and would therefore never again touch the door.

Unfortunately, my ex-inlaws had not been trained to avoid electric wire as Mary and I had been trained. And when they came for a visit a few days later they were NOT pleased to be zapped by the wire. Not understanding the rationale behind putting an electric wire around the front door handle, they called the Department of Social Services (DSS), who promptly came out for a visit.

I was not home when the DSS agents arrived. They were greeted by Mary-the-Donkey in the driveway. Carlene invited them to the main house, which by that time had started to resemble a gigantic dog house. They sat and had coffee with Carlene as the five resident Great Danes hung around looking suspiciously at the visitors.

It was a hot summer day and the agents had mistakenly left their car with the windows down. Mary never missed an opportunity. She reached in and stole their coffee spilling it all over their front seat. At the same time, Rufus was out for his morning walk-about. Freed from the fire alarm obsession, he had developed a new obsession: hubcaps. He became obsessed with hubcaps, so obsessed that we had to park all cars with hubcaps out of sight from Rufus. He would see his reflection in the hubcap and think it was another bird. And Rufus didn't like other birds. He was a fighter and it didn't seem to matter that his opponent was merely his reflection in a hubcap. He was determined to eviscerate his opponent. So, Rufus went to battle on the agent's hubcaps as Mary stretched her oversized head and neck into the car looking for other morsels of food. The agents finished their visit with Carlene and returned to the yard to find their car in battle with Rufus and Mary's head fully submerged in the car.

Despite the five house dogs and vandals' attack on their car, Carlene was somehow able to convince the agents that it was perfectly healthy and normal environment to raise a child.

For a brief period of time, life on the farm passed as normal. I had a normal job. Carlene was less enthusiastic about Animal Episodes and began to think that training service dogs might be less physically challenging than chasing pigs down Storrow Drive in Boston. Turning the new plan to action, she took up the study of training Great Danes as service dogs. Carlene went on to start a nonprofit that provides service dogs to people with mobility problems.

I felt blessed with my life, and often saw that others were far less fortunate. I began to give serious thought to ways I could give back despite my shortage of free time. I needed to find a purpose in life. It took time and searching before I discovered that my purpose was to rescue horses. Once clear on my intent, I started a nonprofit that rescues slaughter-bound horses.

Carlene and I both became fabulously wealthy! Well, not financially wealthy but personally wealthy and very happy with our small contributions to the world.

8. SERVICE DOG PROJECT

Mornings at SDP begin with Carlene head-down in a laundry basket of dog toys looking for a pair of sneakers. She explains that with this many Great Dane puppies underfoot, the best she can do is to define a pair as one right and one left. Matching colors became a figment of her imagination long ago. Obviously her fashion sense has not improved over the years. Next she is off to the

kitchen for a cup of coffee and to the computer to write the Daily Doggie.

The Daily Doggie (or the Doggie Daily) is the way the vast army of volunteers keep in touch with the SDP and happenings on the farm, or at least that was its original purpose. However 10 years after its inception, it has become the random rattling of Carlene who shares her opinions on dog training, world politics, or ponders on the wonders of the universe. Some topics actually lead to lightly funded studies, such as how long will fleas live in a closed plastic bag?

By 7 a.m. the dogs begin to bark, and volunteers arrive, some with muffins (the most valued volunteers bring good food). There are minimal employees at SDP: a kennel manager (Tracy), a trainer (Megan), and a long suffering office manager (Theresa) who tries very hard to keep SDP organized and operating within the confines of the ADI and IRS rules.

The ADI is the Assistance Dog International, a worldwide collection of service dog trainers and advocates who have worked hard to bring together the necessary rules and regulations to manage the business (and the liability) of providing service dogs for people with disabilities.

When SDP was in its formative stage, it became evident that staying aligned with ADI was the best way to go. It seemed excessive for Carlene to enroll in a $5000 training course to learn how to train dogs when it was something she had been successful at her entire life. So before she signed up for the first training course titled 'DOGS SMELL WITH THEIR NOSES," she took 2 dogs, Brownie and Donald, to meet with ADI officials. Both dogs had been used in commercials and were just "generically trained". It was a novel concept to use Great Danes as service dogs. The ADI officials were inspired watching Brownie and Donald work. They agreed that the concept of using Great Danes for service dogs was ideal for veterans returning from Iraq who needed help walking due to a balance issue. Their advice was to continue with whatever SDP was doing and to seek membership and accreditation with ADI.

Great Danes are uniquely suited as balance service dogs. Balance

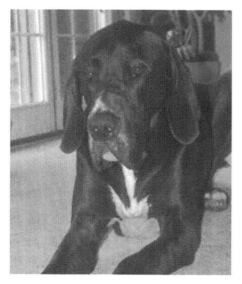

dogs should be at least 45% of the person's height and 65% of the person's weight. In other words, a six foot tall man needs at least a 30" dog. This puts stability at the person's fingertips. SDP dogs are bred specifically for this by incorporating the sturdier European bloodlines rather than the leggy American show dogs.

The temperament of a Great Dane is perfect for this work. They are calm, intelligent and intuitive dogs who do not need much exercise once they are out of the puppy stage. They easily bond with their partner and thus become much more than just a service dog. They often end up being a life line, helping ease the stress and depression which often accompanies disabilities. Danes love the work.

Great Danes are extremely loyal to one person. So loyal, if you have the privilege of being that one person, they will follow you everywhere, including into the shower. You don't need a leash because you always know where they are - right next to you – actually right below your left fingertips usually. They don't shed often, but when they do shed, you will sweep up a pile of hair the size of a Jack Russell every morning. One final concern that applies only to men, is that their tail is like a whip that is exactly inseam height. Otherwise Great Danes are essentially human and naturally make perfect balance dogs.

Contrary to conventional wisdom regarding the lifespan of large breed dogs, Great Danes tend to live to a ripe old age. There are currently three 10-year old dogs still out working and several retired dogs that have reached the age of 14.

Producing the well trained service dogs was not nearly as complicated as dealing with the IRS. To be a member of ADI, an organization must be a 501(c)(3) charity. Having no extra money to pay lawyer's fees, the process of making SDP a 501(c)(3) became a community effort. SDP finally got that magic number from the IRS and gained the ability to accept donations and join ADI.

During this setup time, SDP was blessed with another federal agency—the USDA. The kennels that house service dogs had to be in compliance with the rules with which Animal Episodes had been blissfully unaware for the past 30 years. The USDA inspector was a nice man with a list of things that needed to be done in order to get another magical number that would allow SDP to operate and provide service dogs to the general public. On the top of the list was the six and a half foot wire fence was not in compliance with USDA standards. SDP needed to install the normal six-foot chain link fence with pipe at the top and bottom. It was a simple improvement to install the pipe across the top and bottom of the fence, yet it would cause a number of unforeseen consequences.

On the first morning with the new fence, Carlene stepped out of the shower and heard one of the younger dogs screeching outside the open window. The dog had attempted to go over the chain link fence and got one foot over the bar and the other foot stuck in the chain link. He was hanging from the bar, and obviously very uncomfortable. Carlene rushed out to help, still in a towel and wet from the shower. She was able to get one toe untangled from the chain link fence but it took two hands, leaving no hand left to hold up the towel. The puppy stopped screaming immediately. As Carlene stood using both arms and her head to untangle the dog just as the Fedex truck arrived for their morning delivery. The driver stood speechless for a moment then asked if there was some way he could help. Carlene awkwardly let the dog to the ground and grabbed her towel. When she began to explain, he said "Not to worry. I won't repeat this story. No one would believe me anyway."

The second problem regarding the fence occurred sometime later that afternoon when Deagle (the Stud Dog) reached up with his front paws to the new bar and used it as leverage to catapult himself over. He introduced himself to several female dogs in the adjacent pen and 63 days later he was the proud father of 23 bouncing puppies.

Occasionally fate is a friend. With 23 lovely Great Danes in need of a lofty purpose in life, SDP was off and running and in short time produced its first Service Dogs, "The Merle girls" - Annie, Bella and Maude (all of which are still working at 10 years old).

Annie went to Melissa as a helper with both balance and deafness. Melissa has a great sense of humor and is totally deaf. She delighted in telling SDP that she could not put a patch on her dog that says "Ask before you pat" because Melissa, being deaf, would not hear the question.

Susan uses Maude as a balance dog due to progressive multiple sclerosis. Her husband is confined to an electronic wheelchair due to injuries sustained in the Iraq war. One morning, the wheelchair malfunctioned at an awkward moment and pinned the husband under the bathroom sink. Maude heard him yelling from the bathroom and knew something was terribly wrong. The dog scratched and paced outside the bathroom door and finally realized she needed to go for help. Maude ran through the kitchen and out the giant dog door into the yard to find Susan. Susan immediately noticed that Maude was upset about something and went searching for what that might be. She went into the house and heard Jim's cry for help from the bathroom.

Here lies the difference between training a service dog and training an SDP dog. Service dogs are trained extensively for predefined situations and tasks. SDP dogs are not trained but "educated" to think through situations. In this example, Maude had not been trained specifically on what to do when the husband shouts from the bathroom. In Maude's mental inventory of commands there is no command for "go find help I am stuck under the sink!" One cannot teach a dog to respond in that way. Instead Maude had been trained to think.

ADI was the place to learn so instead of reinventing the wheel SDP joined ADI and went to their annual conferences. One conference was in Florida. Carlene thought nothing of boarding an airplane with a Great Dane. Bailey was a very "useable" dog. She had done many commercials and had a working vocabulary of a 3-year-old child. She tucked right under the seat and slept comfortably on the three hour flight.

The conference was well attended with trainers and service dogs. At one lecture, Bailey was chosen from the audience to come up on stage to help demonstrate techniques on how to train a dog to retrieve a wheelchair. Bailey watched as they rolled the chair 10 feet away. The lecturer continued to speak and make random hand movements, and point several times at the wheelchair. Bailey watched intently and soon figured out that the lecturer wanted the wheelchair back to the podium. She walked over to the rope attached to the chair and grabbed it in her teeth and dragged the chair back to the podium without being given a single command. The lecturer stopped in disbelief. So did Bailey. She had retrieved things before for commercials and movies and always gotten a treat for her effort. Where was the treat? How could this woman not know to give her a treat? Carlene tossed a cookie on the stage and the audience applauded.

The next lecture of the day was on the practical matter of clean-up. A British woman had invented a chunky vomit picker, and other similar gadgetries were unveiled. Carlene made yet another bold move in the face of a large crowd. She raised her hand and asked to demonstrate her clean-up strategy using common household items. She pulled a grocery bag from her pocket and several cardboard squares cut from cereal boxes. She demonstrated how to use the cardboard squares to scoop and the bags to catch. It was an inexpensive, fast, and clean solution to the big problems that Great Danes can create.

While at the conference, a veteran in a wheelchair was heard to say, "Two years of living in war-zone Iraq, I came home injured and they give me this fluffy-girly-dog as a therapy dog. Like that's supposed to help me." He went on to say that although he loved the little dog it was emasculating to lose the ability to walk and to own a dog that only a woman would choose. When he met Bailey, he wanted a Great Dane.

Jim eventually came to SDP and was matched with Homer, a 170 pound wildly colored harlequin Dane. Homer was Jim's loyal companion in harness. He would carefully walk beside Jim through the streets of Boston and stand proudly beside Jim as he

visited many of the local Veteran's hospitals. Homer was so devoted to Jim, he took to growling at Jim's wife. Concerned, Jim called the trainers at SDP. The trainers visited Jim and Homer at their home and were interested by what they found: Homer growled at the wife only when he was in harness. They also observed that Homer would growl at Jim when he was not in harness. Homer in fact adored Jim's wife. Great Danes are highly vocal and it was decided that the growl was not a growl but a grumble. Homer's grumble when he was in harness was his way of saying to the wife, "Can't you see I am working here?" and his grumble when out of harness was his way of saying to Jim, "Can't you see I am off duty?"

The SDP balance dogs are educated to provide independence to their owners. The owners apply for dogs because they are unable to stabilize themselves and often fall. Walkers and canes don't prevent people from falling over backwards, and wheelchairs are an unappealing option. It is amazing to see the resilience and the positive attitude of so many applicants. They all want to walk. They all want to try. Those wanting SDP balance dogs don't want to give up. And they don't want to be confined to a wheelchair. They understand that the dogs are not a perfect solution and will not always prevent the inevitable falls, but the dogs do provide a strong assurance that falls will happen less often, and that the people they serve will be able to get up on their own if they do fall. Steve and Jocelyn demonstrate the joy of independence.

Steve is a typical example of how modern warfare can completely destroy a person's life. Steve went off to war as a handsome, athletic soldier and returned with balance issues and post traumatic stress disorder (PTSD). He rarely left the house for fear that he would fall in public. He became withdrawn and depressed. His wife Rachel was desperate to find help for him and was elated when she heard about the SDP. Steve applied for a dog and after a two week introduction to his new service dog (Brownie) they went home together to assume a new life. Suddenly Steve was a new man. He left the house! He talked to strangers. He laughed, and he loved his new and constant companion.

A month later, Steve, Brownie and Rachel went to Walmart. It was Christmas time and the store was packed with last minute shoppers. Seeing the registers had long lines Rachel took her place in one immediately letting Steve and Brownie wander off in the store together. Heading off, the two passed through the woman's clothing section and only 20 yards from Rachel was where Steve got tangled in a clothing rack and fell over. Brownie could not prevent the fall. The fall created a commotion as clothes tumbled and bystanders either rushed to help or stared awkwardly.

Hearing the commotion, Rachel knew exactly what had happened. For a fleeting second she thought to rush over to help, then the voice of reason prevailed - "Brownie's got it - I am not losing my place in line." And as it happened Brownie did have the situation under control. He'd been taught how to manage falls. He quickly maneuvered himself in front of Steve who by grabbing his harness was able to pull himself to his feet. Smiling at the crowd of onlookers, Steve said proudly "I'm fine, happens all the time."

Jocelyn and Teal are another example of how SDP dogs bring confidence and independence to the mobility impaired. Jocelyn was 13 when she arrived at the farm on the arm of her father. She was completely dependent on an arm of someone for stability to walk. Mostly the arm was attached to her mother or father. She was a normal 13 year-old girl going through growing pains and separation issues like any other 13 year-old girl. What adolescent wants to hang around with her parents? Let alone hang *on* the arm of her parents.

Jocelyn applied for a dog and was matched with Teal. They stayed together in the guest cabin on the farm for a week during the summer. Jocelyn and Teal walked proudly around the farm together. It was the first time in years that Jocelyn had walked on her own. They soon left and Jocelyn returned to school in the September with Teal. At first the giant dog sleeping under Jocelyn's desk disrupted the classroom, but the novelty wore off and Teal became part of the seventh grade class. One day in the cafeteria Jocelyn's feet got tangled. Teal tried to stabilize her but momentum prevailed and both Teal and Jocelyn fell to the floor. For a moment the cafeteria went silent while Teal jumped to her feet. She positioned herself in front of Jocelyn who grabbed Teal's harness and pulled herself up. With Teal she didn't need anyone else's help. She was beaming with joy as she sighed, "I did it."

Over the years, the Service Dog Project placed many dogs with war veterans, chronically ill adults and children. People who had been confined to wheelchairs, walkers or canes have instantly found freedom with their service dog to walk beside. One of the most memorable stories is of Jade, an early recipient of SDP service dog Bristol. Jade had been confined to a wheelchair due to a rare, debilitating, life shortening and degenerative disease called Friedreich's Ataxia. Jade was once an active healthy child before her health and mobility gradually began to decline. By the time she entered her senior year in college she had suffered multiple falls and was confined to a wheelchair. She applied for a service dog and was given Bristol. Together with Bristol she completed her last year of college. Bristol lived in the dorm, went to class and enjoyed life on campus as if she were a student. At the graduation ceremony Bristol looked proud as she carefully walked Jade across the stage.

There is a practical working side of SDP, a side that needs to manage the health, welfare and training/education of over 40 Great Danes. Educating SDP dogs to bond with people and preparing them for a life as a service dog begins at birth. The dogs are handled daily, often hourly.

The training at SDP has not been derived from studying other methods. It is unique to the Danes at SDP and unique to the personality of each dog. You might say it begins 10 days before the puppies are born. Several of the Mother Danes live with other families and come to the farm 10 days before their expected due date so they can relax into the general activity of the farm. The mother dog's temperature is taken daily because there is an old wives tale that the temperature drops from 100 to 98 degrees 24 hours before whelping. SDP has found this to be true - to a point as not every mother adheres to the rule. Regardless, taking temperatures keeps everyone in a state of excitement. A "Delivery Call" list is on the wall for those volunteers who want to attend the delivery. The call list is contacted after the first puppy is born so that there is time before the second puppy is born to gather sleeping bags, coffee and pick up sweet-treats on the way. Puppies are usually born every two hours. With a litter of six or eight puppies, the deliveries can take quite a while.

After the puppies are born and nursing they are weighed and given a name. The two-hour gap between puppies provides ample time for the volunteers to argue over names.

The puppies are then left with their mother to fuss over. Mothers have their own brand of lessons to give. Because Danes are so big, and new mothers are so tired, volunteers are lined up for a 24-hour watch for three weeks. The main concern is that the mother dog does not inadvertently sit on one of the puppies.

At a few days old, the puppies are introduced to a baby bottle with goat's milk. This entertains the volunteers and it teaches the puppies to drink from a bottle. Teaching them to drink from a

bottle when they are not hungry is easy. It is nearly impossible if they are hungry because they are too excited to latch on to the nipple.

At three weeks of age, volunteers grind up puppy food with goats milk, line up dishes, washcloths and a spoon. This is when the real lessons begin. Each puppy is called forward by name and given a spoonful of food. They learn not to push and shove for food but to wait patiently for their name to be called. The feeding-by-spoon is the start of their formal education.

By four months the puppies have learned to follow their trainers, wait patiently, and to get along with other dogs. They are now ready to learn the restraint of a leash. They must learn not to question it. A figure 8 "rope and ring" starts the process with a typical noose around the neck followed by a second loop around the girth. At this point the puppies are so bonded with people that adding a leash is really just a formality.

At six months old the dogs begin their real-world training. Service dogs in training have public access to malls, stores, hotels, and hospitals as long as the dogs are perfectly behaved. Each day the dogs are loaded into a retired ambulance named "Skipper". SDP acquired Skipper on Ebay for $800. The 1984 ambulance had only 16,000 miles on it and was equipped with built in compartments, siren and air conditioning. We celebrated when Skipper passed inspection. Skipper's siren can be heard two towns over. The rig is the perfect transport for the dogs who take a daily visit to the mall for socialization and training. And notably, Skipper is not a vehicle you can easily lose in a parking lot.

The initial goal is to achieve boredom with elevators, checkouts, church pews, restaurant tables, highway rumble strips, sea gulls, exercise machines, kids soccer games, segways, piles of pillows, chipmunks, shopping carts, frogs, air brakes and overly curious people. Once boredom is achieved the business of training proceeds with matching someone's stride, calculating stairs up and down, serving as a brace for lifting a person off the floor, or out of a chair, pulling a wheelchair and just plain paying attention and enjoying the interesting surroundings. These dogs must not snap to attention as an obedience dog is expected to. A service dog must relax and be able to work 24-hours a day. A great deal of time is spent teaching the dogs to be comfortable in public. This is achieved with 'sleeping practice' where the volunteers and trainers spend a lot of time in busy coffee shops. Fortunately our volunteer group is a uniquely cheerful and connected bunch that loves to chatter away at the coffee shop or on the SDP farm.

9. VISIT TO THE SERVICE DOG PROJECT

Visitors to the SDP enter through an electronic gate and are promptly met by Mary-the-Donkey. Her job is to assess the food situation in every car that enters the driveway and solicit treats from its occupants. There is a sign that explains, "This is a working farm and your common sense is greatly appreciated."

The full driveway is over 1,000 feet long which Carlene (at age 74) still plows during every snowfall with an old John Deere tractor wearing a full dark blue snowmobile suit. The same snowmobile suit she bought for me in 1978. As the driveway winds along, visitors will pass two ponds with fountains that are always on. Most people think the fountains add a nice aesthetic touch, but in reality they are on to prevent any algae from accumulating.

Next, visitors will pass a small paddock filled with chickens and rabbits. Who would ever think chickens and rabbits would make good companions? But they coexist very nicely together. At one point the chickens produced so many eggs we kept the neighborhood overstocked. Now the chickens are all so old laying eggs is infrequent.

The final stop is the Ice Tea tent. Carlene spent a summer building the Ice Tea tent, which is not a tent at all, but an open wooden structure with a granite stone floor and fireplace. There are two "Mary-Proof" closets that house snacks and ice tea. The closets are "Mary-Proof", but that is always a temporary illusion because given time Mary will penetrate any obstacle that stands between her and food.

The Ice Tea tent is the core of the SDP. It is where the volunteers and visitors commingle daily with the Great Danes and puppies. There are more couches and beds designated for dogs than there are chairs for people. It is a potluck party that is attended by between 30-50 guests on the weekends and 10-20 on any weekday. It's a diverse crowd. Many physically and mentally impaired people come regularly to spend a little time with their canine friends. The dogs are always happy to greet everyone. The atmosphere is open, pleasant and vibrant. And Mary-the-Donkey is right there in the center of the action either working the crowd for treats or standing quietly among a group of volunteers as if she were part of the conversation. Mary is considered one of the volunteers. Her contribution is to provide goodwill, not attack any of the dogs that mingle innocently between her legs, and not to eat the fingers that feed her carrots throughout the day.

Outrageous ideas are welcome and theories are tested in the Iced T-Tent. One study this summer was on the best way to reduce the flying bug population, mosquitoes in particular. A full under-funded study pursued.

SDP volunteers searched the Internet for answers and it became a playful competition. They hung watered pennies in plastic bags, which didn't catch much of anything. Smeared red beer cups with sticky honey-based "tanglefoot" goop which proved very successful for deer flies. There were many milk jugs with their tops cut off and filled with various concoctions. One was filled with rotting liver (very successful for regular flies), another filled with yeast and dirty socks (worked best for horseflies). Although these methods were effective, neither was highly recommended because of their unsightly appearance and smell. The unofficial winner was a $20 fan blowing air into a funnel of $5 worth of mosquito netting. The mosquitoes and moths were trapped in the net lived very nicely overnight drenched in Raid. This solution made the T-tent and kennels more comfortable for all.

Another T-tent challenge was to humanely solve the issue of unwanted rodents. The containers of dog food and horse grain attract an overwhelming number of rats and mice. I had heard a rumor that Great Danes were used in history to control the rat population in castles in Europe. If that was true, I am not sure what changed over history, because it seems to me that the Danes seem incapable of catching anything. It is fun to watch them try to hunt rats. They are elegant dogs meant to lounge leisurely and clearly not designed to be hunters. Their enormous size makes it impossible for them to sneak up on anything, their attempts to pounce are comical and their pursuit is painfully slow.

The big, well-fed rats were active in the kennels and the barn. They had built a complex network of tunnels underneath the aisle. Our first solution was a cat. We adopted a cat from a local shelter and brought the cat to the kennel to get to work. The poor cat took one look at his new home inhabited by barking dogs and rats that were bigger than him and promptly climbed the ladder to the hayloft. He refused to come down. Finally after two days in the hayloft, a volunteer took him home and adopted him as a house pet. Later, the 'Him' would turn to a 'Her' and deliver a small litter of kittens. Reminding us all (again) that "No good deed goes unpunished."

I took matters into my own hands and decided to drown the rats by filling each rat hole with the hose. I started at one end of the aisle and worked my way to the other end, filling holes along the way. I got halfway down the aisle when I started to see wet rats crawling from the rat holes. First one, then two, then suddenly the entire aisle filled with BIG wet rats, YIKES. I don't like rats, so aborted that attempt.

We tried Have-a-Heart traps. We relocated the rats to the woods. It seemed like the rats would just find their way home again, and invite new rats to the farm on their journey home. So, finally we resorted to rat traps.

We have no deadly chemicals on the property. Therefore the rats were caught in snap-traps. Rats that were caught were promptly bagged and frozen in the freezer in the guest house. They were used to feed the owls and hawks at a local wildlife rehab facility. After the first house guest opened the freezer looking for ice and saw a freezer full of frozen rats, there is now a big sign on the freezer that says "Rat Storage". With a sign like that on the freezer, no one ever dares to open the door. When my son gets a little older, I plan to put a similar sign on the liquor cabinet door. I am guessing that might be far more effective than a padlock.

SDP would not exist without the community of volunteers who do everything from labor to laundry, from spoon-feeding to sh#t-picking. They included the invaluable plumber and electrician who keep everything running, nurses, doctors, and veterinarians to keep everyone healthy, engineers to fix the broken, artists and photographers to capture the moment, and a tug boat captain who keeps the whole crew afloat with good humor.

The SPD attracts committed and loyal volunteers because of its uniqueness. Volunteers check their egos at the front gate and adopt an "all hands on deck" mentality. All tasks are equally important. No one complains about folding laundry, cleaning dirty kennels and there are no personnel complaints either. It's kind of like a family, except everyone just gets along! There is a lot of unexpected fun every day at SDP.

Everything on the farm has a logical design and a practical purpose. Creative solutions to ordinary problems are strongly encouraged. One problem is dog beds. There are 40 Great Danes on the property who all require comfortable accommodations. At any given time, 10 of the 40 are puppies who not only require a bed to sleep on at night but then spend their days biting, tearing and shredding whatever bed was provided. Ordinary large dog beds from a pet store can be shredded and destroyed in a matter of minutes. Couches, twin mattresses and futons have a longer life span in the puppy kennel. At least once a week one gets destroyed and is dragged to the end of the driveway on trash day. I often wonder what the trashmen think about the number of beds, couches and futons they throw in to the garbage truck. They must wonder, "a couch a week?" What happens at 37 Boxford Road?

It would be an interesting conversation if the Trashmen and the Fedex driver ever met.

Once a month, the town offers "Big Trash Day". The volunteers are very busy on Big Trash Day scurrying around town collecting couches, mattresses and futons which fit nicely in Skipper. The most favorable bedding for the Great Danes is futon mattresses (without the frame). The puppies seem less interested in devouring them. SDP had so many wooden futon frames, they began to pile up. One day a volunteer surveyed the growing pile and came up with a brilliant idea. Hay Feeders. The group of volunteers dove in reconfiguring the pile of wood frames into a stack of useful hay feeders for horses. The hay feeders were then donated to the local horse rescue. That's thinking outside the box.

Explore.org

Opportunity came knocking in September 2012 when Explore.org offered Service Dog Project space on their website. The site describes itself as *"a multimedia organization that documents leaders around the world who have devoted their lives to extraordinary causes. Both educational and inspirational, Explore.org creates a portal into the soul of humanity by championing the selfless acts of others."* In a nutshell it is a website where visitors can watch webcams in interesting places around the world. Visitors can watch web cams of the polar bears in Antarctica, grey seals in Canada OR Great Danes at the Service Dog Project.

The cameras are setup around the farm and monitored by a dedicated camera attendant in California. There is a camera to follow the puppies as they play on a grass field called "Puppy Hill" and the nursery room where expectant mothers give birth to litters on live camera. The Service Dog Project on Explore.org has a diverse, worldwide audience that exceeds three million followers. We call these followers the "Camera People" or CPs. CPs are able to add comments and interact with each other online.

The opportunity with Explore.org has been both a blessing and curse.

Explore.org puts everything online, which means everything anyone does is then subject to the scrutiny of the audience. After the novelty of the cameras wore off the volunteers simply forgot they were on camera. These CP's do not miss a thing. They keep track of each dog, person, and piece of equipment- and what we are all doing...

They question everything, from the number of puppies to the

clothing the volunteers are wearing. Because Explore.org is an educational endeavor volunteers try to answer CP questions as best they can.

The CP's are also willing to donate to support SDP. The three million viewers are generous with small donations that go a long way in supporting the enormous costs of feed, vet care and maintenance at SDP.

There is the monthly Chicken Party Game where people donate $10 and are given a number of a square on a table of small numbered squares. On the first Sunday of each month, the SDP holds its Chicken Party. Crowds gather around the small table where squares are displayed. One volunteer goes into the chicken pasture and captures a chicken and places it on the table as the crowd watches anxiously. Usually less than a minute passes before the chicken poops in one of the squares. Whoever purchased that soiled square receives a formal certificate as a member of the *Ipswich Shat-upon Society*. They are also given a cash gift. In the event that the chicken poops on a line thereby selecting two adjacent squares, the poop is careful scooped into paper cups and put on an antique scale. The winner is determined based on the scale's weight.

A 'Fun Fund' involving colored envelopes was started by the CP's. Often CPs see things through the cameras that we don't see sitting physically in the room. CPs are highly involved and engaged in the organization and their opinions and suggestions make a difference in the operation. So the CPs started sending (and are now encouraged to send) colored envelopes with a message of 25 words or less on comments, concerns, or suggestions. These envelopes are opened every day at 5 p.m. and the messages are read. Since the cameras lack audio, one volunteer writes notes to the CPs watching using a white board and pen. Walking in at 5pm to several people sitting around with envelopes and a white board somehow creates the feeling of being on the set of Mr. Rogers. There is just a random, playful and inquisitive feeling in the room (which is often filled with laughter).

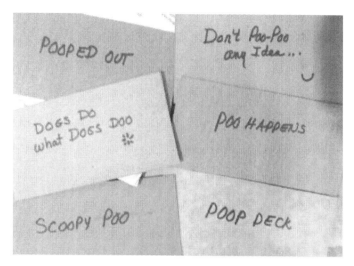

Some of the envelopes we receive are very creative. One CP sends small cardboard squares in batches each month. The squares are to be used as pooper-scoopers. Each carefully cut piece of cardboard has a neatly written note to our volunteers. "Scoopy Poopy", "Poopy Happens", "Don't Poo-Poo an Idea","Scooper-but not for ice cream", "All Pooped Out", "Dogs Do What Dogs DOO" are just some of her messages. It really is little things like this that keep morale so high especially during morning kennel clean-up.

The "colored envelope" concept came about because of the pink envelope campaign to benefit one of SDP recipients in need of help. A student and her dog were not getting the protection from her school staff they were legally entitled to. At SDP's behest the CP Army sent thousands of encouraging notes to the principal and superintendent of the girl's school. Their message could not be ignored and as a result the campaign was successful.

The colored envelope 'Fun Fund' is fueled entirely by pink envelope donations. It is democratically decided what the funds will be used for. This year the "Fun Fund" was used to purchase a full sized tipi, benches, and signage in preparation for the arrival of a large group of CP's who intend to come to the farm in October and meet all the dogs in person.

The CP's add a new element to the SDP. They have become part of the extended family of SDP volunteers. Many CP's have travelled to the SDP farm in Ipswich for a visit. They are always welcome and some have stayed for days in the farm's small guest house.

10. ADVENTURES WITH HORSES

It is evident to me that there is some underlying self-regulating mechanism in my family gene pool that prevents us from recognizing some ideas are simply too big, or require too much work regardless of the benefits. Time and time again, I have watched as Carlene took on some enormous, overwhelming and all consuming project. Each time she threw all her energy into either accomplishing a great thing or writing off another 'Fabulous Failure'. When one project came to an end, she was on to the next. It was a normal circle of life in our family. If she wasn't off on a mission to change the world, she was searching for her next big thing. I heard that the fruit does not fall far from the tree, and in a moment of self-realization, I came to accept that the fruit had actually landed at the base of the trunk. I would rather be excited about the prospect of bringing change or helping to make the world a better place than basking in the luxuries of life.

As I grew older, I began to take inventory of my personal wealth based on the value of accomplishments. I had achieved wealth through academic and professional accomplishments, but had not discovered my ultimate wealth ("working hard to benefit others"). My main interest had always been in horses. Yet, it was several years before I started a nonprofit that would help unwanted ('at risk') horses and ultimately accomplish the type of wealth my family recognizes. I had not found my philanthropic purpose. I knew it must be something that I was passionate about. I saw that my mother had found her personal wealth (SDP) based on her passion for Great Danes and knew my personal wealth was somehow related to horses.

I had been riding all my life and as I grew older I lost the desire to pursue ribbons and discovered new ways to enjoy horses. When I was in my late teens I began fox hunting. Fox hunting is not a competition. It is not a race. There are no ribbons. I rode with a hunt known as a 'drag hunt' where a trail of formulated fox scent is followed rather than an actual fox. There is no killing of innocent wild animals. Hunters in this hunt gallop over hill and dale only in pursuit of adventure and good fun.

Nonetheless our hunt was a traditional hunt. This meant it was required that riders be invited to ride with the hunt and that they arrive spotlessly polished, braided and well behaved. The other riders were from renowned New England families, well bred and poised. Most had grooms to care for their expensive, elegant hunt horses.

I am convinced the reason I was ever invited to ride in the hunt was because I was the only person who could mount a horse from the ground, which meant anytime anyone on the field dropped anything - a helmet, crop or hat I was able to hop off and retrieve it for them. If a gate needed to be opened, a rider fell off, or a hound fell in the river, I was the one to remedy the matter. I knew my place in the field: it was behind the others until my services were necessary. I was not "to the Manor Borne". This I

Janine Jacques
and Carlene White, 2012

understood and was just glad to be on a horse. Growing up as a childhood circus performer did not always lend itself to fitting in with the other members of the hunt. They had all grown up riding perfectly mannered ponies at the country club. I grew up riding ornery ponies bareback in a clown suit. Not quite the same.

Most of the horses on the field were expensive and often imported from Ireland. I have always been driven to rescue horses, so of course my horses were bought from the local slaughterhouse. They weren't old nags, more often they were racehorses that were too unruly to make good pleasure horses after their racing careers had ended. My most notable horse was Cookie, a big, gangly, quirky beast, strikingly beautiful in her own way. If you could not mount a horse while it galloped away, you would never be able to ride Cookie. I bought her from the local meat buyer. He explained that he didn't have the heart to send her to slaughter because she was so young, so beautiful and so sweet - Most of the time. We agreed I would take Cookie off his hands for the sum of $1. Some days I would look back and feel I got ripped off.

As long as Cookie was moving she was quite ride-able. It was the stopping part that she had trouble with. If you were able to get her stopped, she would proceed to rear in place, paw violently and back into the bushes. Fortunately, we had been banished to the back of the hunt field, behind the others, so not many witnessed her explosive nature. Cookie turned out to be one of the best jumpers on the field. When the big Irish imports would shy away from a ditch or unsavory looking fence, she would fly right over and lead the field. It only took one bold horse in front to convince the other horses to follow. In this case, Cookie was not that bold horse, rather I just couldn't stop her. The unsavory fence was just an obstacle in her path to running away with me. I learned just to smile as if the whole thing was a plan.

One day on a hunt, one of the prestigious red coat riders took a tumble and his horse galloped off. Incidents like this were another reason the field of riders would call upon me. They looked to me to retrieve loose horses. I took off on little Miss Cookie and galloped up along side of the loose horse. When I caught up to the galloping horse, I leaned over, grabbed his reins and pulled him to a stop. We turned and trotted back to the horseless rider. I hopped off Cookie and offered him a leg back on to his giant beast. Knowing that I was his only option to get on with the day's hunt, he reluctantly bent his knee and I hoisted him back on the saddle. He was heavier than expected, but I did manage the job. He was also slightly older, slightly handsome and had a strange twinkle in his eye as he trotted away.

Later that day, I received a call from Miles Bishop, the rider. He thanked me for my help and invited me to dinner. I politely declined. I would see him again the next week. He asked if I would like to go out for a ride. At that exact moment, I could not thing of a single reason why not to go…the "Why Not" reason would not occur to me until several years later….

SO I dated Miles for several years. We seemed to share a common theme in life and pursuit of crazy adventures - or at least he was a good follower. We came from different worlds, but then again, it would be difficult to find someone with a background similar to mine. Like many relationships, everything was perfect at the start. Miles had appeared self-supportive and accepted a "less is more" lifestyle with me. We biked, hiked, rode our horses, visited the local pub, and shopped at Costco together. Miles even bought a motorcycle so we could bike together. Life was simple, normal.

However a year into the relationship, Miles began to encourage me to regularly have my nails, toes and hair done. He preferred my hair blonde instead of brunette. As soon as I had completed the transformation to a blonde with sparkly red nails, he began to encourage me to evolve socially.

I never learned to cook a thing. It's a limitation I inherited from Carlene. Carlene was so defiant in her domestic responsibilities, once my father suggested she do more cooking at home. The next morning she removed the stove from the house, dragged it down the long driveway and put a "FREE" sign on it. It was gone by noon. Sometimes Carlene would worry the children were not well nourished so she would send us to the garden for half an hour to eat peas. She timed us with a stopwatch. Given my role model, it is no wonder I have been domestically challenged.

I did grow up knowing proper manners and good graces. I did know which fork to use for salad, which for the main course and to keep my elbow off the table. I knew a proper dinner guest is gracious and always offers to help the hostess in the kitchen. But while other guests might offer to help in the kitchen *before* dinner, I thought it best to assist with clean up *after* dinner. It was my contribution to a dinner party. Everyone loves to cook. No one likes to clean up. I loved clearing the plates and helping the hostess prepare dessert. Miles was slightly embarrassed when I would collect everyone's plates around me after dinner and politely excuse myself to the kitchen.

I think the final nail in the coffin of my relationship with Miles, was my bargain hunting ways. In this, I considered myself gifted. I pride myself on being a stealthy, renegade shopper in the constant search for the perfect deal. It is difficult for me to pass a consignment store, my car automatically slows at the slightest sign of a garage sale, and nothing makes me more elated than scoring a 'good stuff cheap' bargain. I love to talk about my retail accomplishments. If someone compliments me on an article of clothing, I proudly tell them the price and how much I saved. I would say, "Normally this Loro Piano blazer would be $2300 online or in their Park Avenue store, but I found it in the $6 dollar bin at Gentry's Consignment in Newburyport." For stealthy shoppers like me, paying full price for anything is a failure. It lacks creativity and commitment - and it definitely doesn't make good dinner conversation.

One night we attended a fundraising gala, a lovely black tie event. I was so excited. I had the perfect dress: a full length, fitted dress with a high slit up the side. Simple yet elegant - it originally sold at Nordstrom for $995, but I found it at the Salvation Army in Wellington, Florida for $15. So excited....

I was pleased when Miles's eyes lit up when he saw me in my 'New-to-Me' dress. As we mingled through the crowd, I received many compliments. In my mind, I did look fabulous, plus I was now blonde and definitely feeling more fun than ever. When we sat down to dinner everyone at the table complimented me on my dress. I was so proud. It was too much for me to hold it in any longer - I blurted out that I had bought the dress at the Salvation Army for $15 dollars. I was glowing. The table went silent but I did not. I quickly changed the conversation and began talking about the adventures of Mary-the-Donkey, Rufus, and Crazy Acres. Soon everyone was erupting with laughter. Everyone, except Miles.

Several days later, Miles explained to me that sadly I was just too common for him. We parted ways. For several months he would call late at night to say he missed me, and us. How sweet, but I was too busy living my very common life to take his calls. One thing about circus performers, we don't stay down long, and our show must go on.

After the break up, I decided to allocate one week for each of the three years we had dated to a "Dating Moratorium". While I had planned to mourn the relationship for three weeks, I really felt better after three days.

The lesson I learned - it is WAY easier to get two masters degrees, a Ph.D., train a cockatoo not to make fire alarm noises, catch a reindeer on the State House lawn, gallop on a horse in a chicken suit, and out run angry bulls than it is to find a suitable life companion. Since I have been fortunate to always be surrounded by animal friends, I don't think I will ever know how it feels to be lonely or alone.

11. HOPE4HORSES

I found my purpose in life and my "personal wealth" when I learned the hidden and dirty little secret about the horse industry. It all began on Facebook.

Social media and Facebook have impacted people in many different ways. For me, signing up for a Facebook account changed my world in a way that I never would have imagined. I was late to adopt social media because I didn't see the point of sharing photos and posting comments until I noted that my sister had 128 friends. I suddenly realized that Facebook was a popularity contest. I had failed the popularity contest when I was an awkward teenager and had no intentions of failing this modern day popularity contest on Facebook. I created a Facebook profile and became a Facebook slut – friending everyone and anyone. I was elated when I saw my number of friends growing beyond that of my sister.

Then I saw a post from a complete stranger whom I had friended on Facebook. It was a post that would change my life. She wrote that 130,000 horses went to slaughter in Canada and Mexico. What? I was certain that we had abolished slaughter in this country in 2007. It never occurred to me that American horses were simply shipped across the border. I went on to read her lengthy post about the deplorable conditions for slaughter-bound horses. I was immediately inspired to help in some way.

I started by friending people on her friend list. My network began to grow and was leading me to learn more about the slaughter industry and also more about how I might take action. I found there is a group in Pennsylvania that takes photos of slaughter-bound horses and posts them on a Facebook page. I saw that the followers shared the photos, offered homes, made donations and were helping to rescue these horses.

I noted that the horses posted were not just older horses going to slaughter but young, healthy horses. I wondered how nice horses could possibly be unwanted and slaughter-bound. I researched only to discover that these horses are merely another symptom of a new economy and the changing (shrinking) horse industry.

Horses were treated differently when I grew up. The horses were turned out in big pastures together. They ate grass, drank out of a stream and came into the barns only when it was cold. Horses are herd-animals. Together they ran and frolicked in fields. They sowed their 'Wild Oats' running with their stable-mates which made them more reasonable to handle and ride.

Riders were different back then too. There is a big difference between "growing up riding" and "taking riding lessons". There were no worries of lawsuits and liability. Children rode bareback. They rode their horses in the woods, through fields and spent less time trotting around in circles in a ring. Children who grew up riding were not so fearful of falling off. Riding bareback on ornery ponies trained them to fall off and get back on because "involuntary dismounts" were just part of horsemanship.

On our farm the children 'grew up riding'. It was a process of accumulating experiences both on and off the horse. For most, it began at a very young age. Children under 6 were closely managed. Parents were told that the distance between parents and children under 6 must equal the child's age. Therefore, if a child was 5, the parents must be five feet away from their child at all times. In addition, children under the age of 6 were not allowed to ride with a saddle. This not only taught young riders good balance, but also avoided dangerous accidents where kids get caught in the saddle during a fall.

Children over 6 were given a helmet with an elastic strap and off they would charge to play Cowboys and Indians in the backfield on well-fed ponies at high speeds, often falling off several times in a single day. We did have one riding lesson per week to learn proper equitation in the saddle. Beyond that, children were trusted to use good judgment in pursuit of good fun.

Central to "growing up with horses" was horsemanship. We learned to think like a horse and anticipate their actions, to know when they would be fearful, aggressive or cooperative. Understanding the subtleties of horse behavior was particularly important during dinner time when **one** person would have to carry **one** bale of hay into a field of 14 horses. The hay was to be spread in a large circle with a flake for each horse. Although it appears to be a simple task, spreading hay into 14 piles while 14 hungry horses gallop around was daunting. The horses would argue with each other over who was the first to the hay pile. The horses would kick and sneer at each other while I would quickly distribute hay into the 14 piles. Hooves flying, ears pinned and teeth bared, my biggest fear was getting caught in the crossfire. I studied the pecking order and knew that Tacky would kick at Harvey, Harvey would kick at Bingo, but Bingo would never kick at Tacky. Strategy was important as my safety depended on which horses were within firing range. The best defense was to move quickly and yell loudly at all of the horses. The adage "Allies are people with common enemies" applies to horses. You were in grave danger if you weren't prepared to be the "Alpha Horse" when you opened the gate carrying the single bale.

Many of today's equestrians would get pummeled in that field of horses because they haven't learned the nuances and subtleties of horse behavior. Regardless, horses are not turned out in herds like that anymore. Real estate is so expensive that the big farms have been sold off and the surviving farms have downsized. As a result, rolling pastures are a rarity. Instead, horses are kept in stalls and turned out in small paddocks for only several hours a day. Horses are typically turned out alone because of fear of injury. It's not much fun to frolic alone, so after a few minutes they stand and wait to be brought back to their stalls. Also their diets have changed from eating self-serve green grass all day, to eating hay and "high octane" grain. Many riders even feed supplements to their horses to promote good nutrition.

SO here is my idea of the perfect storm that is brewing for horses:

- Today's riders take lessons and are less connected with the horses they ride.
- Most riders spend time trotting around in circles in the ring, and less time allowing their horses to move forward and burn off excess energy.
- Horses are kept inside, fed high energy diets then brought out to open riding rings for a trot-around. Since most horses don't have the opportunity to frolic, some simply frolic under saddle, tossing their riders in the playful exchange. "Sowing Wild Oats" has real meaning.

- Suddenly paying $300-$1000 per month to keep a horse doesn't seem like a good idea when you are frequenting the emergency room with injuries.
- The last part of this perfect storm is the new economy. Americans are shying away from big purchases, especially ones that require monthly feed, veterinary care, and new shoes every six weeks. Therefore, selling horses is increasingly difficult. Selling a horse that bucks off its rider on occasion is near impossible at any price. Unsold horses eventually fall into the precarious category of "Unwanted Horses."

I started Hope4Horses Equine Rescue in 2009 as a means to help unwanted horses. It's estimated that there are over 160,000 unwanted horses in the United States, and my initial goal was to help 12 unwanted horses per year. It was an aggressive goal to rescue, rehabilitate and rehome 12 horses, but I recruited a close friend and 5 board members who were inspired to work together to meet this goal. We applied for a 501c3 status with the IRS and began purchasing slaughter-bound horses.

In January, 2010, we rescued the first group: 3 young horses and 2 mules. I had seen photos of them on Facebook. They looked sad, unwanted, and in need of groceries. I hired a hauler to transport the horses from New Holland, Pennsylvania to Palmer, Massachusetts.

The hauler's name was Spud. I had spoken to him several times on the phone and agreed to meet him at his farm in Palmer early in the morning to pick up the horses. When I drove up the long driveway the next morning, I had no idea what to expect. The long driveway was lined by broken down fences, broken down cars and broken down tractors. A big antiquated barn stood at the end. Out came Spud, surrounded by a pack of motley dogs. He was scruffy, bearded and looked like a dusty old cowboy. He was very pleasant and had a slight smirk on his face.

Spud led me into the barn where all three horses stood together in one stall. The three horses were yearlings. Emaciated and tired, they hovered together, a pathetic looking group with runny noses and hacking coughs. "They'll be nice horses, if they survive," he said flatly. Spud was a true cowboy, whose advice stemmed from first hand lessons he had learned the hard way after a lifetime being surrounded by horses. So I valued his opinion – especially when it came to the fate of these horses.

The three yearlings were only half of the problem. The other half were the two mules: flashy, pony-sized mules with four white stockings that reached their knees. The mules were fat, healthy and still in the trailer. Spud explained he left them in the trailer because they were not halter broken and appeared wild. I peered

into the trailer and saw their big brown ears. They were so awfully cute, how could they possibly be so wild? There was a halter on each mule with a loose lead already attached. I instructed Spud to grab one lead while I grabbed the other, and we would pull them over to my trailer. He refused. "They are stronger than they look. I got things to do and don't wanna be chasing mules all day, all over town." He turned quickly, jumped in my truck and backed one trailer up to the other. We then chased the mules off Spud's trailer onto mine. I could tell by the exchange that Spud was right, these mules were wild!

With everyone loaded, I headed back onto the interstate toward Boston. It was rush hour so I soon ran into traffic. My mind was fixated on Spud's comment "if they survive" when I heard a loud thump from the trailer. I was convinced one of the horses had fallen over and died. I put my blinker on and I started to pull over. Since it was rush hour in Boston, no one was going to let me change lanes in a truck and trailer. Then it occurred to me, I was alone with three sick horses and two wild mules in city traffic. What would I do if one had died? I had no answer, so I drove onward without stopping.

I arrived at the family farm. The farm was filled with volunteers who were thrilled to see the new mules. I was just thrilled to see all three horses were still alive. Carlene peered in and saw the mules with halters and leads dragging on the trailer floor, "You grab the bigger one, I'll grab the smaller one," she said.

"Oh No, they are wild, I will back up the trailer and we will chase them into the barn." I answered. Somehow Carlene managed to convince me it was a good idea to try her plan.

Carlene kept the trailer door closed just enough for me to slip in and grab the lead ropes of each mule. When I had both leads in hand she opened the door. The mules stood quietly. I gently tugged the lead. Nothing. Carlene came in and grabbed the second lead. She gave a gentle tug. Nothing. We pulled harder and tried to lure them with grain, but those mules were not getting off the trailer.

All else had failed, so I got the broom out of the trailer. I gently touched the mule with the brush-side of the broom. That seemed to do the trick and off they went, knocking Carlene over and dragging me along. One mule was loose instantly. I had a firm grip on the other. The mule ran off with such force I fell to my knees and then my stomach. I held on tight with both hands unwilling to give up and let go. After being dragged for 30 feet on my stomach, it occurred to me the battle was lost. Reluctantly, I let go and sat up to watch as the little mules sprinted around the property with Carlene on a golf cart following closely behind. I didn't panic knowing that the entire property is surrounded by a split-rail fence. Once we got them cornered, I was confident we had the situation well under control. But panic returned when both mules jumped the four foot split-rail fence from a standstill and ran off into the neighborhood. Memories of chasing reindeer and my pony Tinker dragging the wheelbarrow flashed through my mind.

We chased those mules all around the neighborhood before we finally chased them up the driveway, through the open gate and into the barn. It was a rude awaking to the world of rescue. It suddenly occurred to me that the horses (and mules) that I planned to rescue were unwanted and had been discarded by the horse-community. I am not sure why that hadn't occurred to me before the mule incident. I thought back to my days living with Rufus. He was unwanted in a nunnery, yet I managed to figure out a way to fix him. I just needed to think creatively with each rescue and devise a plan for how to convert every *unwanted* horse, donkey or mule into a *wanted* horse, donkey or mule.

The mules were three years old, unhandled and untrained. It took three weeks of constant handling and contact with humans for them to realize that humans were not so evil after all. Grain helped. At every meal, I would sit with a bucket of grain and wait for their hunger for grain to outweigh their fear of humans. Waiting patiently has never been one of my strengths, in fact it is a well documented weakness. I tried to use the time productively. I would sit by the bucket of grain for hours reading the book, "How to Start an Equine Rescue." I figured it was never too late to read the directions.

It took one hour and 12 minutes for the braver of the two mules to slip his nose into the bucket of grain at my feet. Within days the mules were eating from my hand and following me around the paddock. They realized I was a source of food and not a source of concern. It was then time to introduce them to the rest of humanity. I put a general notice on the wall for all farm visitors "DO NOT WALK PAST THE MULES WITHOUT FEEDING THEM BY HAND." Underneath the notice was a full bucket of grain. The only problem was as the mules grew friendlier, they also grew fatter! Fortunately, there was a market for slightly obese, flashy little mules. They found a home on a gentleman's farm in Pennsylvania and have fully embraced their new role in life as lawn ornaments and affectionate pets.

Spud was right, the three horses in the trailer were very, very sick. Two had pneumonia and required 24-hour care for two weeks. The third had a six-inch long gash along the inside of his knee and was not too keen on having it wrapped. After a daily 20-minute argument to get him to stand quietly to get his knee wrapped, I would put him back in his stall where he would become instantly obsessed with the play-toy I had strapped to his leg. How fun it was for him to pull and chew the bandage! The process of ripping and unraveling usually took about two hours, three if I added defensive measures like duct tape. I even tried to design a cone thingy that they put on dogs, but he ate that too.

In the end, everyone survived, except me. Rescuing the horses,

93

nursing them back to health, and finding them homes was both physically and financially draining. It was too much to manage all the moving parts in my life. Working fulltime, being a fulltime mother, and rescuing horses stretched me too thin. I felt frazzled and unfocused. I had to rethink how I could help unwanted horses. I needed to find an effective executable plan that leveraged my passion, energy and skills. Since my business and academic expertise is technology that became my starting point.

12. EQUINE RESCUE NETWORK

It took me many years to figure out that struggling to improve upon my weaknesses was futile. I had always thought of myself as a hard core equestrian; willing to ride anything, jump high fences and muck stalls. That clearly was not reality. Now older, perhaps slightly wiser and more educated, I found I was not the equestrian I once thought I was. I came to the realization that I was definitely not the equestrian that I needed to be to care for rescue horses.

I remember when I was in my teens, I told Carlene I wanted to be a professional rider and equestrian. I was talented (enough to stay on *most of the time*), experienced and willing to work hard to accomplish my goals. Carlene was not as excited about my future as I was. She explained I was to go to college, earn a degree and then I could do anything I wanted with my life. Her work raising (and funding) her children ended the day I graduated from college. She explained, "College will make your brain a more interesting place to live." There was no negotiating. I was going to college. It was made clear that I was to get myself *accepted into* a college and *graduated from* a college. I was not to go to a college within 200 miles of the house because she feared I would come home with my dirty laundry on the weekends. My college would be paid for with the expectation that when I graduated I was on my own financially. Starting the day after my graduation, I would not only have to support myself, but also my two horses. It all seemed a little unfair, but off to college I went.

I studied business where I learned to run numbers, how to balance a budget and make sound financial decisions. Suddenly, I realized there is no sound financial decision that would lead a rational person to own horses. Someone once said, "Owning horses is a good way to make a small fortune out of a large one." I decided it was best to focus on making a large fortune. Computer professionals were in high demand and some were making large fortunes, so I decided to major in Computer Science. I graduated in 1988 and had a handful of job offers. Since my end goal was to own horses and make a small fortune out of a large one, I chose the job that paid the most.

After years of office work, I have discovered I am far less hardy than I once was and my vision of rescuing horses is just something I am no longer cut out for. It was a sad moment when the last of the five rescues went to a forever home. I had a fleeting moment of pride thinking that I had saved their lives. That moment was immediately followed by a sense of failure in that I was not willing to rescue anymore.

How could I still do something to help horses? I had thought my purpose was to rescue horses and I had lost my purpose. And I felt having that purpose was both beneficial to horses and essential to my own internal well-being. I always feel better doing good deeds to help others. It's funny, people often give me accolades for my philanthropic pursuits. What they don't understand is my philanthropic efforts are for my own well-being not for mankind. Helping others makes ME feel better about ME. I am no saint donating time and money to worthy causes. Rather I am a selfish lost soul seeking purpose and sanity in my crazy world. Honest, but true.

I was not willing to give up. If my purpose was to rescue horses, there must be other ways to accomplish this without long hours of barn work and horse care. I thought about how I learned about the slaughter of American horses and how it had excited my passion to help horses. It dawned on me that there must be others like me who want to help. I thought if I could bring these people together and convince everyone to give a little time, money or support we might be able to save a few horses.

After a rocky start with several failed attempts, I finally figured out a sustainable business model and launched an electronic campaign through Facebook in September, 2012. My mission was to benefit 'at-risk' horses by bringing equine advocates together electronically on a page called the "Equine Rescue Network" (ERN). The ERN includes both social media pages and an interactive website.

I waited patiently and watched the number of followers slowly grow to just 441 followers by November 1, 2012. I was discouraged that all of my hard work and enthusiasm had led to another dead end. Yet I was still unwilling to give up. Years of farm living and circus performing had taught me that FAILURE IS NEVER AN OPTION.

I kept trying until I finally hit the social media jackpot and devised a media campaign that attracted attention. It was a simple advertisement that said "IGNORE this Ad if you don't want to help slaughter-bound horses, LIKE us if you do." The ad generated 42,000 likes in six months.

With 42,000 likes I was able to raise the money needed to rescue 32 horses between January 2013 and March 2013. We raised an additional $27,000 dollars to help the equine victims of the 2013 Oklahoma tornado tragedy. That was all good, but if you think outside the box, envision big changes, there are more ways to help the growing population of horses.

One way is encourage horse owners to microchip their horses. This way we could identify microchipped horses when they enter "at-risk" situations and reunite them with previous owners. Ideally there will be a simple phone app that would be accessible to animal control officers, auction houses and veterinarians. For example, if a horse were found abandoned or abused, law enforcement could scan the microchip and enter the number into their phone app. The app would retrieve all contact numbers of previous owners. The owners would then be notified and asked if they would like to be reunited with the former horse.

Another way to help horses (and dogs) is to encourage pet-sharing. This is a great idea. I have experienced pet-sharing first hand. I personally believe it has value in creating a sustainable world for our animals.

13. LOVING LIFE, LOVING ANIMALS

I remember when I was a kid, Carlene received a call from the local dog pound (back when shelters were called 'dog pounds'). There were two dogs scheduled to be euthanized. They asked (begged) my mother to see if she could help them. SO off we went to the dog pound. The two dogs (obviously littermates) were big, young dogs that were unruly to handle. Not mean, just too strong to hold on a leash and hyperactive. I remember Carlene being dragged down the hallway by the two dogs that appeared less than a year old, well fed and a cross between a Great Dane and a Newfoundland. She stuffed the two big, fluffy dogs in the back of her yellow Volkswagon bug (with a Rolls Royce hood) and drove home. It was a bit dangerous to drive with the two big dogs bounding playfully around the back seat. My job as the passenger was to keep the dogs in the backseat so they didn't land in the front seat and obstruct Carlene's view as the driver.

We made it home safely and unloaded the dogs into the house. It was an immediate disaster. The dogs just could not contain their energy level. They were completely untrained and not house broken. Obviously this is why these two dogs were doomed to euthanasia at the pound. Some dog owner had decided to breed their Great Dane with a Newfoundland, enjoyed them as cute puppies, and dumped them when they became too big to handle. Sad, but TRUE

An untrained dog is an unwanted dog.

They were like Thing One and Thing Two in the Cat-in-the-Hat, creating complete destruction everywhere they went. One would grab a shoe while the other lifted his leg on the coffee table, then bound up the stairs, jump onto the nearest bed, grab a down pillow and dart off to the hallway leaving a cloud of down feathers along the way. If you tried to catch them to contain them, they would jump on you knocking you over, and lick your face when you were on the ground. These dogs were too big to be this out of control. They must have weighed over 130 pound a piece. We couldn't let them loose outside because they would surely run off. The first night the two dogs spent the night in the barn where they howled all night. Their training began in the morning.

I watched the next morning as my mother began their leash training. These dogs were so big and strong, it was almost impossible to hold them on a leash. They would dig their back legs in, put their head down with such determination, and drag you off with the force of a bull. Carlene first took a strong webbed collar and leather leash, which they immediately chewed through. Next, she replaced the leash with a chain and tied each of the dogs to a tree 20 feet apart. It took two of us on each dog to get the dogs out to the trees. The dogs fought the chain and collar for at least 1/2 hour before they finally settled down.

The next day, she took the same collars and chains and devised a quick release link and attached each dog to the seat of the golf cart. I stood on the back of the golf cart (where the golf bags normally stand) holding the end of the quick release rope. Carlene drove off very slowly while I called the dogs to follow. They were smart dogs and soon realized the 'game' was to follow the golf cart. Being oversized puppies, they loved games and with their big fluffy tails wagging, they bounded after the cart. Soon they settled into a nice steady trot as Carlene headed to the back field which had a track that we used to gallop the race horses in the mornings.

This became the routine. Coffee in hand, we would head out to the backfield with the dogs every morning. It may seem like a crazy idea to use a golf cart to run two dogs around a track every morning, but it was the 1970s and how else would we contain these two grizzly-bear-sized dogs? We would drive slowly around the field for at least a half an hour, drinking coffee while the morning sun rose over the trees.

The first day we had to wrap the rope around seat as leverage while I stood on the back watching the two bear sized dogs trot along. The most amazing part of our morning routine was the dogs went from unruly monsters to reasonable dogs almost instantly. After two days, we no longer needed to wrap the rope on the seat, because the dogs knew what was expected of them: they were to trot behind the cart. By the end of the first week, no rope was needed. They just followed the cart and didn't have any aspirations of running away. Carlene explained:

A tired dog listens better" - "A tired dog is a good dog"

These dogs just needed exercise. They were young dogs, bounding with energy and cooped up at the dog pound. They needed to run - and they did run every morning for the first few weeks.

Carlene worked with them in the afternoons, teaching them the simple boundaries and expectations on the farm. In short 5 minute lessons, they had learned the lesson of the leash. Next, they learned simple lessons about boundaries, restrictions and expectations. They learned to listen and not fight. She talked to them as if they were human at times. They would sit patiently and stare intently back at her as if they understood every word she was saying. Carlene became Alpha in their world. They learned quickly how to be good dogs and nice pets. After three weeks, they were awarded the privilege of roaming freely on the farm. They were normal farm dogs and like the rest of the occupants of the farm, they knew their place and what was expected of them. The dogs got plenty of fresh air and exercise. They had found their permanent home and their place in the world. When we went out in public with the pair of dogs, Carlene would often get compliments on the beautiful dogs. In reality, they were *just average dogs that behaved beautifully.*

Those two dogs were lucky. Over 4 million dogs a year are not so lucky. They don't have a Crazy Carlene to step in and save them from an untimely doom. They don't have a person who will give them the time, training and the fresh air they need to be good dogs in a not-so-dog-friendly world.

Love your dog, train your dog and provide them with a good life.

Did you know that wild dogs can travel up to 30 miles a day? Contrary to domestic dogs who travel on average less than one mile. So if you own a dog, you will need a pair of comfortable shoes and may even consider taking up jogging as a new sport because dogs need to run and according to leash law dogs need to be on a leash when they do.

Towns are too quick to pass leash laws in my opinion. I do see the value in having a leash law. However, residents don't realize they are condemning the dogs in their town to life at the end of a leash.

When they pass a leash law in a town, they should also make provisions for a dog park in that same town.

You don't have to go to a class and march around in circles to train a dog. Every time you handle an animal you are training him. It doesn't take any great effort to develop communication with your dog. The most important training technique is consistency.

My dog is Thumper. I am fortunate that Thumper is perfectly trained. I wish I could take the credit for that, but I can't. He is a "Fabulous Failure" of the SDP. He has just a few marginal quirks that made him unsuitable (unreliable) as a service dog. Most notably, when he gets scared, he runs. Fortunately, it doesn't happen often but all it takes is a car to back-fire or the loud crash of Thunder and he will run for cover, knocking over innocent bystanders. Beyond that, Thumper is just perfect. If he were not, I would invest time in training him.

I believe all dogs can benefit from training. I further feel it is the owner's responsibility to train their dogs, and if they are unable to train their dogs, they should seek help from a professional dog trainer. Untrained dogs (just like horses) become "at risk" and often end up being "unwanted" or have limited lives.

Here is an example:

I try to take Thumper on a walk every day. I can't say that I get him out every day, but most days, Thumper (like many Great Danes) has an extreme aversion to inclement weather so he will only go willingly if the sun is shining and the day is warm. I recently ran into my neighbor and I was surprised to see her walking a small dog. I stopped and admired her new dog, a cute long haired brown Terrier mix. He was very excited and bouncing around at the end of the leash. "What a cute dog" I said as I reached down to pat the happy little dog. "When did you get the new dog?"

"Oh, he is not new." She answered. "I have had him since he was a puppy. We keep him in the backyard because he's not good on a leash. He pulls - it's annoying." We exchanged a few more neighborly pleasantries then I walked onward.

How is it possible that I didn't know my own neighbor had a dog? I never see her walking a dog. I know everyone on my street that owns a dog because I see them *with their dog* – at the dog park, on the nearby trails, and in their cars. This poor little terrier didn't get out much. How sad. Why not invest time in training and teach him how to be a better dog? I called a friend who trains dogs for a living. I got his card and put it in her mailbox the next day. I haven't seen her walking her dog since.

A dog that pulls on a lead is no fault of the dogs. The problem is at the other end of the lead. Who wants to walk a dog that yanks them around on a leash? It's a simple fix: tell him not to yank you around. They stay consistent. I have seen Carlene stand somewhere with a dog. The minute he pulls, she pulls him back near her and immediately releases. She essentially told the dog that she expect him not to pull her around. Then she stays consistent with her message and soon the dog doesn't pull anymore.

Depending on the willingness and intelligence of your dog, you may have to tell him several times, but most dogs for the most part dogs want to please. Then it's all about CONSISTANCY. Every time you have that dog on a leash you are reinforcing the expectations you have set. By the way, many would argue the same is true for children. I know it is true for both dogs and horses.

DOGS PRAYER:

"Treat me kindly, my beloved friend, for no heart in the entire world is more grateful for your kindness than mind.

Don't be angry with me for long. Don't lock me up as a punishment. After all, you have your job, your friends, and your entertainment. I only have you." ~ Anonymous

I recently came across the 'dog's Prayer' and was momentarily overwhelmed by 'dog guilt'. If you are a dog owner (or actually any pet owner) you will understand what I mean by 'dog guilt'. Maybe it is just the way I am wired, but I feel guilty if my dog's day is not full of fun, exercise and fresh air. But I have a life too. A life that is often not conducive to owning a dog, especially a big dog.

My first problem is my car. I have a mini cooper and a Great Dane (Thumper). It's a problem of "too much dog, not enough car" but he seems to be happy stuffed in the backseat. The problem is with my son in the passenger seat and Thumper in the *entire* backseat, there is not room for anything - no room for groceries, other children, gym bag or dry cleaning. I would really like to take him everywhere. Mostly because when left behind, Thumper has perfected a combined look of horror, shock, disappointment, and agony, so the dog owner guilt is overwhelming. The reality is there are many times when he is left behind.

The second problem is my job. I have one, and I have to go to that job in order to support my life which includes the expense of Thumper. I tried to explain this to him, but he just doesn't seem to like the fact that I leave him – ever.

I remember the days (not so long ago), that I would pack up for work and leave our two dogs outside loose for the day. There was no leash law in my town. The dogs knew not to go near the road. They had a dog house to shelter them from the cold and rain. They had each other. I never felt guilty. I have no idea what they would do all day, but I would return from work in the evening and they would be happy and tired.

Things are different now. Owning a dog is a much greater responsibility. You are not only responsible for the dog's nourishment and care, but you are also his only access to the outside world - and he must be on a leash.

"Time is the only true currency"

My third issue with Thumper (and my life) is time. I have discovered the truth in the saying "time is the only true currency." It seems that everyone in this new digital age is overcommitted, stressed and time constrained. I don't know anyone who has 'free' time. I personally have come to accept that Time is actually NEVER free. It comes at a cost to something. Time allocated to work, is time divested from fun. Time allocated to fun is time divested from professional development or income opportunities. Time allocated to spend time with Thumper is time divested from all of the above. Although, time with Thumper is most relaxing and rejuvenating; nonetheless, it is still in lieu of time spent elsewhere.

Fortunately, I found a solution to having a happy dog and permanent relief from 'dog-guilt', I "Dog Share" Thumper with another family. It's a perfect solution. I met a nearby family that really wanted a dog, but felt their lives were too disjointed to take on the fulltime responsibility of a dog. We discussed the options, Thumper's needs, and his training. We worked out a schedule.

Now I go off to work and he goes to the Wilson's house to play with their children, ride around in their minivan, and take a leisurely walk after dinner. Sometimes he sleeps over the Wilson's house if I am travelling or out for an evening. They bought a bed identical to the one I have for Thumper.

Thumper understands the drill. Like a child of divorced parents, when the Wilson's drive up Thumper's bag is packed and he is waiting at the door. He has learned to love the Wilson family. He gets excited to see them at the door. Like most dogs, Thumper is overflowing with love and affection so he has plenty to give us all. Now, instead of Thumper's sad face when I leave for work, his tail is wagging and he is off to the Wilson's.

I met the Wilson family by chance, but I have since learned there are many, many online pet sharing sites that make it possible for people to connect. Like everything else in the new millennium, we need to rethink and redefine pet ownership. There are solutions out there that will help address the enormous population of unwanted pets. Using microchips to create accountability for breeders and pet sharing are two solutions that I personally believe could have a big impact on the lives of many animals.

"He gave me a happy life, I gave him a happy life, Then he went to sleep"

The end of this chapter is related to end of life. Chances are you will probably outlive your pet. When I watched my dad grow older and eventually die at the age of 94, **I realized there is no way easy way to get from this life to the next**. People must suffer through the agony of terminal illnesses. My father was approaching death and suffering for months before he finally died. The last few days were augmented by hard-core narcotics, but it still was some-kind-of-awful, that I am not looking forward to in my far away future. Hopefully, by the time I start to fade, people will have options the way that we have for animals.

Although it is sad when animals die (actually when anything dies) it is far worse when animals suffer. Euthanizing a terminally ill or aged animal is a far better solution than letting them suffer.

Every domestic animal has one goal in life. That goal is to find one human to love them enough to give them the education and care they need to be good companions. Baby animals are a blank slate that we need to develop into good pets and companions. That is our job on this planet as human occupants! As animal lovers, let's not ignore that responsibility.

14. LESSONS FROM ANIMALS

If personal wealth is measured through accomplishments and giving back, how can you build your personal wealth to achieve success and happiness in your own life? There is no generic answer to this question. Your personal wealth is unique to you and only you can find and build your fortune. However, there are two key elements that will provide insight and encouragement for anyone interested in managing their personal wealth.

The first element is perpetual motion. You will not find your purpose unless you go out into the world looking for adventures and embrace hard work. Think big, dream big, look outside the box and set goals every day, every week, every year. Work towards these goals tirelessly. Accept that you will not meet all your goals but recognize that working towards them is a far better life strategy than having no goals at all. Adopt a philosophy of movement both mentally and physically. And never stop looking for the reason you landed on planet Earth.

The second element is to listen to the world around you. People need us. Animals need us. Yet, some people choose to ignore this need and focus on themselves. I am not so certain that true happiness can be attained with an egocentric attitude. I have made a choice to focus on rescuing horses. I feel this is well suited to my passion and expertise. What are your skills and passions? How can you combine and apply them to benefit others?

I will close with several inspiring stories. These stories inspire me to broadcast a message about animals. I feel the world will be a better place if I can inspire others, the way that my life has inspired me to do more and give more.

A dog is the only thing on earth that loves you more than he loves himself. — *Josh Billings*

My first story is begins at a low point in my life. Very low. I was sick. Fortunately I am seldom sick, but when I am, I am a disaster. As you can imagine having Carlene as a mother does not lend to having a sympatric, motherly ear. She can always trump me with some more catastrophic ailment. She is like a war horse. She had polio as a kid which resulted in Scoliosis of the spine; then a head injury that caused her to develop epilepsy and migraines; plus she is older so her random aches & pains far exceed mine. Therefore, when I get sick I am on my own.

One common theme between Carlene and I is that illness does not deter us from a full day of activities. We may be a little slower, complain a little more, but a day of bed rest just doesn't happen in my family.

On this particular day, my to-do list included a trip to Home Depot for Spider Repellent. I own a rental unit that went unoccupied for a period of time. Well, unoccupied by humans at least, it seemed the neighborhood spiders saw the vacancy sign and moved right in. My tenants complained about sharing the residency with spiders (rightly so) so I went off to Home Depot for a solution to that problem.

I was feeling so awful that I stopped into CVS to buy a

thermometer on the way. I figured if I had a temperature someone might actually listen to my constant whining. I bought a thermometer and being the impatient person I am, I need to know my exact temperature right away! The electric thermometer was enclosed in an impenetrable plastic container that was designed to withstand a hurricane. So I brought the thermometer into Home Depot. God knows they have power tools, they must also have scissors.

I was pleased to find scissors, except they also were enclosed in an impenetrable plastic container. No problem, I went up to the service desk and ask them for scissors and where to find some spray to kill spiders. The woman behind the counter was so sweet; she opened the thermometer container and told me I should go right home to bed. Sometimes sympathy from a random stranger is all you need...

I put the thermometer in my mouth and walk over to aisle three. I was pale, sniffly and everything ached. When I am sick, I don't care what I look like or if I have a thermometer hanging from my mouth at Home Depot. So there I stood, thermometer in my mouth, overwhelmed by an entire isle dedicated to killing things. I am one of those crazy people who relocates spiders with a glass and an index card. I don't obliterate them with spray. My other problem was that I didn't have my glasses so I couldn't read any of the writing on the packages. I couldn't be bothered to wait for a person to walk by who actually worked at Home Depot, so I just grabbed the next random person who walked by and asked them to read me the description on the package.

Around the corner came a man pushing an orange cart. I didn't even look at the man, just jumped at the chance, "Can you read this package for me? Will it kill spiders?" I mumbled through the thermometer in my mouth. He took the plastic bottle from my hand and stared at it closely for a minute. "Yes, that should work" he said. "But, let me give you some advice on Spiders, I am an exterminator by trade so you asked the right person…" and he began a long dissertation on how to control spiders. In the middle of his advice, I had to stop because the thermometer was beeping. I had a temperature of 103 degrees.

Despite my raging temperature and even without my glasses, I noticed that this man was not well. He just had everything wrong. He was short, with a distended belly worse than any pregnant woman that I had ever seen. He had a red face, long grey hair that began from behind his ears. There was no hair on the top of his head. His teeth were yellowish brown, crocked and there weren't a lot of them. He was wearing sweat pants and old sneakers. As he drew closer in the conversation, I noticed he was a bit smelly too. Now, I am never one to judge, especially in the condition that I was in. I always feel badly for people like that. I know what it feels like to not fit in with the world. I envision his life as sad and lonely. He had no wedding ring on and probably lived alone. I felt sympathy for the poor man, and waited patiently while he described how to kill spiders.

Then he made a remark about his dog. He had a dog - Thank god! Suddenly my moment of sadness and sympathy dissipated. He was not alone. He had a dog! I asked him about his dog. His eyes lit up as he explained how he had adopted the dog from the local rescue – an older dog that went everywhere with him. "I don't have a problem with any critters in my house - She chases spiders and anything else that doesn't belong in my house." He said proudly. "She is in the truck waiting for me, just swung in to pick up a few things. Here's my card if you need any more help, but you should be fine" He said as he pushed his cart onward down aisle three.

My point in this story is that dogs and animals don't have the same shallow minded hang-ups that we have – or maybe I should just say *that I have*. Thankfully, *animals do what our society often does not - they love everyone equally despite awkward and different appearances*. They don't judge or discriminate and base their judgment on what is inside a person.

I rushed home and climbed into bed with Thumper. He never gets to sleep in the "Big Bed" with me unless I am sick. He jumped right up – not caring that I was a mess, or that I didn't feel good. He just cuddled up with me happy to be close and at my side.

"The greatness of a nation and its moral progress can be judged by the way its animals are treated." *Mahatma Gandhi.*

My son is now 14 years old. I am not sure what age kids should be trusted to ride the subway alone. He had an appointment in the city and I had things to do, so I decided the appropriate age was 14 and dropped him off alone at the subway station during rush hour. My final words of advice were, "keep money in your front pocket, use your Iphone for directions, and if you need help ask a woman who looks like a Mother. Mothers always help other mother's children."

I pulled out of the T-station and turned left into heavy traffic. I continued along to the first intersection where I immediately noticed chaos. There were cars honking and slowly diverting around the center of the intersection. People seemed to be ignoring the traffic-light entirely. I thought there must have been an accident, maybe a pedestrian? As my car rolled closer to the intersection, I saw the root of the congestion. A small flock of ducks hovered in the middle of the intersection. You could tell the poor guys were terrified. There were 12 of them. They looked to be ducklings barely old enough to be on their own. I assumed their mother had just recently separated from them as ducks do when the ducklings get to an appropriate age. I envisioned somewhere there was a mother duck that had just launched her small flock out into the world. I imagined she may be feeling like I was, probably worried and hoping that all she had told and taught her ducklings would be enough for them to live safe and healthy lives. If she only knew the fate of her poor ducklings at that moment.

I was amazed that the traffic just slowly diverted around the ducklings. No one got out of the car to help them. The ducks would turn sharply in unison every time a car passed. They went from one direction back to the other. Since they were surrounded by cars slowly passing by, they were stuck in the center of the intersection. Some drivers appeared slightly annoyed at the inconvenience the ducklings were causing. Others smiled as they slowly drove by marveling at the little creatures. I wondered how we had become a society of passive participants. Here these animals clearly were in distress yet no one took action.

"The world is a dangerous place to live; not because of the people who are evil, but because of the people who don't do anything about it" *Albert Einstein.*

I jumped from my mini cooper and trotted into the middle of the intersection. I herded the little ducklings with the precision of an Australian sheep dog. The ducklings responded and seemed relieved to be given direction out of the chaos. They huddled together moving in unison. I moved them across the intersection into an adjacent parking lot.

Now that the crisis was averted I looked for the best place to leave the flock. I noted that there was a park across the street with a large pond way off in the distance. It was probably where they came from and should return to. To the dismay of the four lanes of traffic, I began to move the ducklings back across the street. I had years of experience herding animals, and the ducklings at this point knew I was trying to help them, so the move was efficient. Yet one angry man shouted at me from behind the window of his air conditioned car. I continued onward with my flock and together we trotted safely across the intersection. Jumping up the curb, the ducklings waddled off toward the pond and their new life

Minutes later I received a text from my son. He had arrived safely at his destination in the city.

I headed to my office feeling a sense of accomplishment on that blazing hot day in August. I had left my dog (Thumper) inside my air conditioned house for the day. He is a big black dog that doesn't do well in sweltering heat. It was too hot for him to venture far from the house. I know he is perfectly content sleeping all day in the cool house but I feel he needs to get out, get exercise and spend quality time with me every day. I returned home from work early to take him down to the river for a swim.

Through the woods behind my house is a small park with a wide, deep river and a small beach for swimming. Most visitors to the park drive in through the main entrance but since it is so close to my house and admission is free, I walk to it through the woods.

On that day the river was full of swimmers of all ages and sizes. When I arrived the first thing I noted was an extremely large (very obese) man walking toward the river. He walked slowly. In his hand were two lit cigarettes. When he got to the river, he waded up to another large (very obese) woman and handed her a cigarette. And there they stood, up to their chests in the cool, refreshing water smoking cigarettes.

I am not one to judge anyone so I dove right in followed closely by Thumper, who waded into the river and stood proudly with the water up to his chest.

Great Danes don't swim. I used to try to encourage Thumper to swim. I would drag him out in to the water above his head hoping he would catch on to the "doggie paddle". Instead he would panic, flail about and try to climb up on anything that would prevent him from drowning, which was usually me. His size and big paws almost drowned me on several occasions. As a result of several near drowning experiences, Thumper and I have come to accept that he is not a swimmer, but a wader. On that day, he stood peacefully as I paddled out to the middle of the river just ten feet away.

Everything seemed fine in the river until the police showed up on a random patrol. The officer jumped out of his car and marched down to the river and shouted, "Get that dog out of here, dogs don't belong in this river!" then turned and walked back to his car. He said nothing about the couple smoking cigarettes.

Thumper followed me as I walked out of the river. On the shore I paused to dry myself off and noticed the smoking couple extinguish their cigarettes in the water and throw the cigarette butts into the brush by the shore. Funny what is now considered appropriate in nature.

I stopped on my way past the bush to pick up the two cigarette butts. I don't like when people throw cigarette butts on the ground. I imagine that some fish, bird or turtle will try to eat the butt and die an immediate death from cancerous nicotine. I know it's an irrational thought, but I picked them up and threw them in the nearby trash can. I stop for turtles on the road too and wish more people would do the same. There is a safe way to grab a turtle between the front and back legs where there is no danger of being bitten. My only advice if you are going to save a turtle, make sure you are all-in when you grab the shell. As soon as you pick them up from the roadway their little legs start moving. Don't panic, don't get scared and drop the turtle, stay focused on your mission - that turtle's life is in your hands. Dash for the side of the road and don't get hit.

My point is we need to find a better way to protect animals in a sustainable environment. We need to discover animals' place in an evolving society, whether it is dogs in the river or turtles crossing the road.

Let us never forget the positive role that animals have in our society. They love us. They entertain us. They teach us valuable lessons. And some even help us walk! My only hope is that our society will continue to recognize the importance of animals on this planet and in our lives.

Our animals need our help. We need to listen to them, learn from them and help create a better world where we can coexist peacefully.

15. DOGGIE DAILY (APPENDIX A)

I have a love hate relationship with the Doggie Daily, which is distributed by email and viewable as a blog. Many people read the Doggie Daily every morning religiously. How many, I don't know exactly but I suspect a lot. I love to read it, yet hate when I am a subject in the Doggie Daily. I never used to read the Doggie Daily. It would pop into my email box every morning but I was just too busy to take the time to open it until I met a random couple in Gloucester, Massachusetts.

I was standing at a bar of restaurant waiting for a table and having a martini. I started talking innocently with a couple next to me who were also waiting for a table. After fifteen minutes of enjoyable conversation, I introduced myself. "My name is Janine."

She remarked, "Janine, now that is an unusual name. How do you spell it?"

"J-A-N-I-N-E" I replied.

"My name is Mercedes, another unusual name. I like unusual names. Don't most people spell Janine with an E after the J-A?"

"Yes, that's the French way of spelling Jeanine" I replied. "I like to think of myself like Tigger, I am the only one that spells it J-A-N-I-N-E" I said jokingly.

"I know someone else who is also a Janine and spells it the same way." she said "Well, actually, I don't know her. I follow a blog and she is frequently mentioned in the blog."

Suddenly it dawned on me. NO! It couldn't be. I reluctantly asked "Is that blog called the Doggie Daily?"

And suddenly it dawned on her "Oh my god! *You are* Janine from the Doggie Daily! I read about you all the time! I love to read about you. Your mother is so funny."

Oh dear, I was "*Janine from the Doggie Daily*" to a complete stranger. I know Carlene and I know her sense of humor. I know she likes to entertain her audiences and that my misfortunes and mistakes are far more entertaining than my accomplishments. From that point in time, I started reading the Doggie Daily every morning.

I quickly learned that it is true. I am a popular and frequent topic in the Doggie Daily. For example, the day I forgot to pull the emergency brake in my standard-shift-car and it rolled down the hill, through a fence - that made the Doggie Daily. The day I got caught by one of the Explore.org cameras P-ing in the barnyard - that made the Daily Doggie. When I was left hanging from a tree on the hunt field and my horse galloped home without me - that made the Doggie Daily.

Her exact comment in the Doggie Daily was "AGAIN I WAS REMINDED WHY I TRAIN DOGS NOT HORSES. SOMEHOW JANINE WENT OUT FOX HUNTING AND ENDED UP HANGING FROM A TREE IN HER POLISHED BOOTS AND FANCY BRITCHES. THE HORSE CAME HOME WITHOUT HER. I AM NOT SURE HOW THAT HAPPENED,

BUT AT LEAST THE HORSE HAS ENOUGH SENSE TO GET
HOME SAFELY. BY THE WAY, GREAT DANES WOULD
NEVER LEAVE YOU HANGING LIKE THAT" – The real story
is that I took a young horse (an ex-racehorse rescued from
slaughter) out fox hunting. It all started out fine, but suddenly the
little horse bolted off into the woods leaping and bounding. The
horse came to a dead stop abruptly; I assume to avoid crashing into
a large tree in his path. He flew back into the equine-equivalent of
'reverse.' He was backing up so violently his legs got tangled and
up he went into a full rear thrashing awkwardly as his front feet
rose.

It's amazing how quick your mind and body react in situations like
that. The horse was obviously going over backwards. My mind
must have known this and told my arms to reach up and grab a
branch from a tree. The only thing I remember flashing through
my mind was "oh shit" – and next I knew I was hanging above the
horse as he scrambled to his feet and took off toward the golf
course. The branch wasn't quite strong enough and buckled under
the weight of my body. I landed gently among a sprinkling of
leaves. It wasn't until the next day that I realized those leaves
were poison ivy.

The horse galloped across a golf course on his way home (I know
this because I received the bill from the golf course for the damage
to the green). With the navigational skills of a homing pigeon, he
trotted through town, a state park and eventually up the driveway.
Carlene found him standing quietly at the front gate. I was still
wandering around the woods looking for him when Carlene called
my cell phone to let me know he was in his stall.

It's refreshing to know that I am not the only family member that
provides a source of entertainment for the Doggie Daily. I did note
that my sister (Gwen) made the Doggie Daily which caused all
sorts of drama.

When I talk about the "the fruit falling from the tree" and the "Crazy Carlene Gene", I got a full dose of crazy, Gwen's dose was only slight. She is, for the most part, normal. So normal, she rolls her eyes when she is faced with evidence of the shenanigans of either Carlene or I. She is married, balanced and has a normal job; a big job, lots of people to manage, responsibility, and stress. To relieve her stress, she sometimes shops. Having no time to shop offline, it's mostly online on Ebay.

Gwen would wake up stressed and sit at her computer shopping for tidbits, collectables and shoes late at night. Boxes would arrive - many boxes – so many boxes, so many random things, and too many shoes. Finally, her husband shut her off. Reluctantly, she agreed *no more Ebay*!

That promise didn't last long. One night she was having difficulty sleeping so she found herself in a familiar spot – shopping on Ebay. She impulsively bought a pair of Jimmy Choo shoes for $225 – NIB (new in box) that would normally would for $995. It was a score she just couldn't resist.

The next morning she was in a panic. How could she pay for the shoes, get them delivered without her husband finding out? She called Carlene and explained her dilemma on her way to work. Knowing Carlene's fashion sense, she was unsympathetic. Yet, somehow they agreed that the shoes would be delivered to the farm, and Carlene would pay for the shoes. In exchange, Gwen would clean the chicken coop.

Gwen woke up the next morning, dressed in a suit for work, kissed her husband goodbye and went on a clandestine mission. She drove across town to the farm. She stepped out of her fancy car, removed her expensive, tailored suit and put on the blue snowmobile suit. Next she covered her head with a shower cap, grabbed a wheelbarrow and shovel, and disappeared into the chicken coop for several hours. The chickens all waited patiently outside. It was several wheelbarrows full before the coop was clean and fluffed with fresh bedding. She came out of the chicken coop, took off the snow mobile suit, shower cap, back into her suit and off to she went to the big city for work.

It was a perfect plan with one slight oversight. The Doggie Daily! The next day the Doggie Daily explained the whole scenario including the Ebay shoes and shower cap. Gwen was horrified - and her husband Ron, well let's just say after 20 years of marriage he has come to expect random incidents where the 'Crazy Carlene Gene' is to blame.

Despite my own personal reservations of the Doggie Daily, it is a good source of dog training and life tips. It is entertaining and often inspiring to many. I have included some of the more recent ramblings. The content is unedited because part of the charm is the misspellings, capitalizations and butchery of punctuation.

Hope you enjoy.

Very random ramblings of life at the Service dog project

DAILY DOGGIE – UNEDITED EDITION

Latest news - DANE NAMED QUIETEST BREED OF DOGS. I HOPE SOMEONE REMEMBERS THAT WHEN MY NEIGHBORS TRY AND JAIL ME AGAIN. the story on vetstreet.com

Mary--- (ALL 750 POUNDS OF HER) visiting inside Brooksby Village yesterday could not have been better..

with her feet duct taped so she did not catch a carpet thread--- we wandered THRU THE GLASS DOORS down the hall to a large "living room" sort of place where 35 or so patients in wheelchairs waited to see mary.

polly's friend had proviDed her small fry pan and patients held the pan while bob put a few carrot slices in it and mary happliy chomped away-- working from wheelchair to wheelchair.

SHE QUIETLY WALKED IN A CIRCLE CASING THE JOINT FOR THE NEXT FRY PAN WITH CARROTS.

I WONDER WHAT HAPPENED WHEN THOSE PEOPLE TOLD THEIR FAMILIES THERE WAS A GREAT BIG DONKEY IN THEI MEETING ROOM.

i would never do it with a horse... but MARY WAS AS GOOD AS BAILEY EVER WAS.

JODY'S TRAVEL COMPANION - MARTHA- SWUNG INTO PLACE AS KEEPER OF THE PAIL OF CARROTS'

****

WE HAD A BOARD MEETING--LAST NIGHT AT THE IPSWICH COUNTRY CLUB- BECAUSE OF THIS DAILY DOGGIE NOT MUCH NEW WAS DISCUSSED-

PERRILS OF TRYING TO FIGURE OUT WHAT DOG WOULD BE BEST WHERE ---IS ALWAYS A QUESTION WITH NO ANSWER- BUT WE TALKED ABOUT IT.

****

I HAD A LAST MINUE BRAINSTORM AND ASKED THERESA TO TRY AND COME IN 1/2 HOUR EARLY- TO LOOSEN UP MEGAN AND I TO ADD A TRIP TO THE FAIRGROUNDS WITH PUPPYS FREE RUN..

AND WE ATE.

****

PAUL THE PLUMBER IS GOING TO CONTACT "CARPENTER JIM" AND SEE IF HE CAN FINISH UP SOME DETAILS ON THE NEW NUT HOUSE- IT WAS SUGGESTED I GIVE JIM THE 50 CENT TOUR OF PIECES OF KENNEL LYING AROUND WAITING TO BE INSTALLED.. MY GOAL OF TRYING TO HAVE A " HOSE DOWN" PROOF KENNEL IS MAYBE A NEW THING FOR A NORMAL CARPENTER. AND PAUL LIKES WORKING WITH HIM LEARNING NEW TECHNIQUES... LIKE THAT METAL BENDING JERRYRIG DEAL.

****

I WISH OUR HOUSE WAS PURPOSEFULLY TILTED - WITH A DRAIN... WOULD SAVE ALOT OF HEADACHE !.... AND LAUNDRY.

****

POOR LUMPY MARQUE IS STILL WAITING FOR THE RESULTS OF THE BIOPSY-

HE SEEMS CHEERFUL ENOUGH BUT HE LOOKS SOOOOO BAD THAT IT IS HARD TO PAT HIM WITHOUT RUSHING TO WASH YOUR HANDS.

IT CAN NOT BE CONTAGEOUS- OR MORE WOULD HAVE IT-- - THERE IS ONLY HIM.

****

AND BOBBY WITH THE SWOLLEN PRIVATE PARTS

I WAS TOLD GEORGE GOT 240 CC's OF GOOP OUT OF THEM- WITH A BIG NEEDLE- APPARENTLY A VERY BIG NEEDLE (PER MEGAN)

CONSEQUENTLY THERE IS CONSIDERABLY DRAINAGE--- AND AS OF LAST NIGHT BOBBY DOESN'T FEEL GOOD-- WOULD NOT EAT- SO WE HAVE THAT TO DEAL WITH THIS MORNING.

****

MAY 30th

TRAINING AND THE GREAT RACE ARE ON SCHEDULE FOR TODAY'S TOPICS.-

TRAINING IS COMMUNICATION-- AND THE BEST HUMAN EXAMPLE OF IT IS IN THE OLD MOVIE <u>MIRACLE WORKER</u>-- ABOUT HELEN KELLER- WHEN AS AN IMPOSSIBLE AND DESTRUCTIVE CHILD SHE ALL OF A SUDDEN REALIZED THOSE HAND MOVEMENTS MEAN "WATER"

DOGS GET TO THAT POINT WHERE THEY REALIZE YOU ARE TALKING TO THEM AND PAYING ATTENTION IS A GOOD THING..

THAT NH CRONICLE SHOW LAST NIGHT (GOOGLE WMUR TV SERVCE DOG SHOULD GET ITI) GIVES A GREAT EXAMPLE OF WHAT WE STRIVE TO DO IN THE FINAL STAGES BEFORE HARNESSING. GO AND HAVE A LOOK -- THERE IS ONE SEGMENT WHEN MEGAN IS WALKING THE ONE STEP WITH LOLA-- AND LOLA TURNS AND LOOKS UP AT MEGAN WITH THE "HAVE I GOT THAT RIGHT NOW?" THEN AGAIN WITH MURPHY ALL OF A SUDDEN HE COMES AROUND HER LEG AND LOOKS UP WITH THE SAME LOOK. "WOW I DID IT RIGHT"

FAST FORWARD TO WATCHIING JOCELYN AND TEAL WORK TOGETHER AND SEE HOW OFTEN HE VERY SLIGHTLY TURNS HIS HEAD TO CHECK ON HER REACTIONS..

THERE IS ALSO A GOOD DEMO OF WHY NOT TO TALK TO A SERVICE DOG - WHEN THE REPORTER SPEAKS TO JOCELYN AND STICKS OUT HER HAND...., FOR ONE SPLIT SECOND TEAL TURNS TO HER AND THEN IMMEDATELY BACK TO JOCEYN AND HIS JOB... BUT THE INTERUPTION IS OBVIOUS.

***

THE OTHER THING ... IF WE ARE USING OUR MUSCLES TO CONTROL A DOG WE ARE DOING SOMETHING WRONG. I AM NOTED FOR YELLING/SCREAMING/ SPEAKING VERY LOUDLY------ ABOUT A LOOSE LEASH-- AND THOSE TRAINING COLLARS NEVER SHOULD HAVE BEEN CALLED A CHOKE CHAIN-- A VERY UNFORTUNATE NAME- COLLARS ARE ANOTHER TOPIC FOR ANOTHER DAY.. BUT LOOSH LEASH IS THE RULE OF THE DAY

ON THE FARM MOST OF OUR HANDLING IS DONE WITH THE DOGS RUNNING FREE.. STARTING WITH THE PUPS RUNNING AFTER MEGAN.. FOR THE ODD TIMES WE HAVE A SPECIAL PROJECT LIKE--- TO KEEP 2 MALES FROM ARGUNG .. WE USE A COTTON ROPE WITH A LOOP.

THE TRAINING COLLAR IS A CONVERSATION TOOL-- IF YOU NEED IT FOR CONTROL, YOU HAVE SOME HOMEWORK TO DO.

----- STANDING OR MOVING THAT LEASH SHOULD NEVER BE TIGHT.

IN THAT VIDEO I DID NOT SEE ANY TIGHT LEASH(I JUST WENT OVER THE VIDEO AGAIN TO BE SURE.)

YOU WILL SEE JOCELYN TIGHTEN HER LEASH- THAT WAS

UNPLANNED- BUT AS WE WORKED ALONG WE REALIZED SHE NEEDED IT FOR BALANCE- AND AS LONG AS THE LEASH WAS BACK ON TEALS SHOULDERS HE WAS FINE WITH IT . SHE WEIGHS 57 POUNDS AND TEAL ABOUT 150- IF SHE CAN'T CONTROL HIM WITH HER VOICE AND BODY LANGUAGE, SHE IS IN BAD TROUBLE. BUT TEAL LOVES HER

THIS WILL GET ME IN HOT WATER....

A PROPERLY TRAINED DOG WILL ALLOW YOU TO CARRY A TRAY OF 4 CUPS OF COFFEE IN THE SAME HAND AS YOUR DOG'S LEASH WITHOUT SPILLING A DROP..

****

THEN THE GREAT RACE.. *OR WHY SHEILA AND I HAVE SO MUCH IN COMMON....*

I MAY NOT HAVE THE DETAILS RIGHT- BUT WITH THE GREAT RACE IT DIDN'T MATTER.

I THINK IT BEGAN AS AN ARGUEMENT BETWEEN 2 GUYS IN MATTY'S SAIL LOFT- A BAR IN MARBLEHEAD-- WHETHER IT WAS FASTER TO GET FROM WATERTOWN TO MARBLEHEAD FASTER BY LAND OR BY SEA.. ?26 MILES?)

THAT TURNED INTO MANY THOUSANDS OF NEARLY SOBER- VERY CREATIVE PEOPLE PEDALING ODD VEHICLES OR CARRYING CANOES ON THIER HEADS ALL OVER BOSTON AT 4AM.

IT ENDED WHEN THE IRS FIGURED OUT THE THOUSANDS OF T SHIRTS COST $5 AND SOLD FOR $15-- AND NOBODY HAD THE PROFIT. !

IT WAS GREAT WHILE IT LASTED ?5 YEARS?

THE WINNER WAS ALWAYS DISQUALIFIED BECAUSE THEY MUST HAVE CHEATED.

I DID CROSS THE FINISH LINE FIRST ONE YEAR -- ON THE PENNY FARTHING BIG WHEEL BIKE. I BEAT DAVE MAYNARD BY 32 SECONDS-- HE HAD SAILED A WATERBED...

NOW I FIND OUT THAT SHELIA COMPETED ONE YEAR IN AN 8 PERSON BIKE ALL WELDED TOGETHER INTO ONE VEHICLE- I REMEMBER AND ADMIRED THAT VEHICLE- AND I SAW A REPLICA OF IT IN ?HAMMERCER -SCHLEMER? CATALOG -- IT WAS A 8 OR 10 PERSON VEHICLE WITH 8 PEDLERS SITTING SIDEWAYS AT A BAR LIKE RAIL.

*THAT GREAT RACE WAS A MARVELOUS INSTITUTION. IT
WAS ALSO NOT EASY- FROM MY STANDPOINT-- THAT HIGH
WHEELED BIKE HAD NO BRAKES- THE ONLY WAY TO STOP
WAS TO RUN INTO SOMEONE AND FALL OFF WHICH MADE
THE 26 MILES A GRUELING PROPOSITION.*

*SHELIA-S CONTRAPTION WAS A DIFFERENT STORY'- THEY
TOO MANAGED TO CROSS THE FINISH LINE BY HANGING
ONTO THE VARIOUS PIECES OF BIKE THAT HAD COME
UNWELDED.*

*THE LAST RACE FINISHED ON THE BEACH IN NAHANT (
MARBLEHEAD RESIDENTS GOT TIRED OF CONTESTAANTS
UNABLE TO FINISH FOR ONE REASON OR ANOTHER...) I
WAS IN THE CROWD WHEN 6 GUYS ON FOOT TOWING AN
ANTIQUE FIRE HOSE. ON MONSTER IRON WHEELS
CRASHED THRU THE FINISH LINE, SIDE SWIPED AN
EXPENSIVE CAR AND CRASHED INTO THE LINE OF
PORTAPOTTIES-- THE POLICEMAN JUST TURNED AND SAID
"HOW THE H3LL AM I GONG TO WRITE UP THIS REPORT?"*

I HAVE OFTEN THOUGHT OF THAT REPORT..

*THAT CREATIVITY IS NEARLY DEAD KILLED BY EITHER THE
LIABILITY INSURANCE OR THE IRS...*

DARN SHAME (GOOGLE TED KEN ROBINSON)

****

SO BACK TO OUR DOGS AND TRAINING METHODS

WE GOT THE PANDORA REPORT AND MUCH THE SAME FOR DAMIEN.

Hi Carlene and Crew,
Just wanted to comment on your training for the CP out there that have doubts. Pandora is one of Carlene's Danes and has come to our home in NY to become a therapy dog. She was in a litter before the cameras so very few know about Pandora. We have continued the training Carlene started. With only a couple of weeks with Pandora I realize I have NEVER had a dog this well trained. She walks by our side, lays down, stays, waits, comes, leaves it and more. What ever Carlene and her crew are doing is working. Pandora is going to make a fantastic therapy dog, she is going to make an impact on many lives. Thank you Carlene and please don't change a thing.
Debbie

THANKS GO TO ALL THE VOLUNTEERS WHO HELPED PUT PANDORA TOGETHER.

TODAY SCHEDULE?

*SOMEBODY GOES AND SOMEBODY COMES AND THAT S
ALL I CAN REMEMBER-- BECAUSE WHATEVER IT IS, IT WILL
ALL HAPPEN WITHOUT MY HELP*

*MAYBE BECKY WILLBE BACK FOR ANOTHER SOAK IN
MYNEW BATHTUB.. TRACY AND MARIA ARE ALL SET TO
TAKE ADVANTAGE OF THE PEEP HOLE IN TE BATHROOM
WALL WITH THE EXPLORE CAMERA*

STAY TUNED

Saturday, August 10, 2013
AUG 10, 2013

*IN MY "STABLE OF ADVISORS"- ONE OF MY MOST
RESPECTD\ED IS 'NOTHER GWEN" FROM EDINBURGH-
NOW LIVING IN BELFAST. SHE USUALLY CHIMES IN AT
CRITICL MOMENTS-- AND TODAY I GOT THIS...WEE NOTE.*

*Good to read that bit in the blog about an Apple. I love ours and it
surprises me that none of my contacts here have one. I find it far
easier to use than the old PC and it is so much faster.*

SHE HAS A WAY OF BEING RIGHT...-- GWEN IS THE ONE

WHO WANDERED AROUND GERMANY WITH ME FOR A WEEK LOOKING FOR DANES..

(I THINK I TOLD THAT STORY RECIENTLY----- ARMED WITHA ZIP CODE LIST OF KENNELS AND A RAIL PASS- WE JUST GOT ON ANY TRAIN AND THEN TRIED TO FIGURE OUT WHERE WE WERE GOING.)

ON THE TOPIC OF COMPUTERS-- I SHOULD PLAN TO SPEND SOME TIME AT APPLE ON MONDAY AND GET SOME HEAVY DUTY DECISIONS MADE...

ALL BECAUSE THE DESK INTHE OVERFLOW ROOM IS UNCOVERED THANKS TO SHELIA'S ATTENTION TO DETAIL.

THERE IS NOW PROBBLY A 9 DAY WINDOW WHERE IT WILL REMAIN UNCOVERED---

PLAN IS TO MOVE THIS BEAST IN THERE AND INSTASLL THE APPLE EQUIPMENT HERE

****

NEXT PROBLEM IS WILLIAM HUBER---

I DO NOT KNOW WHAT HAS CAUSED HIM TO BE FIXATED ON PUTTING A DOG ON A STUMP IN A SWAMP FOR A PHOTGRAQPH PROBABLY FOR THE NEXT CALENDAR-- HE HAS WANTED TO PHOTOGRAPH THAT FOR AT LEAST 3 YEARS... WH OAM I TO QUESTION IT?? BUT LET ME TELL YOU IT WILL BE EASIER TO PHOTOSHOP OPAL'S SPOTS ONTO BAILEY THAN IT WILL BE TO GET OPAL ON THAT STUMP..

AND THAT IS SUPPOSED TO HAPPEN SUNDAY AFTERNOON-- LATE-- HAS SOMETHIGN TO DO WITH THE TIDE ALSO...

SO THERE WILL BE SOME ACTIVITY AROUND HERE WITH STUMPS AND DOGS IN THE PARKING LOT--- IF WE HAVE TO USE BAILEY, WE WILL HAVE TO CARRY HER THRU THE SWAMP--- SHE IS DOING REALLY WELL - BUT FOR THIS-- SHE GETS CARRIED-

KITTY HAVE YOU RUN ALL THIS BY MEGAN AND OTHER HEFTY HELP? I CAN'T DO "CARRY" AND ABOUT THE STUMP---- IS IT 2' HIGH OR ACROSS...?

THERE IS NOT ANOTHER DOG ON THE PROPERTY WHO HAS HER PERSPECTIVE ON WORKING.. FIGURE IT OUT----- PUT UP WITH ANYTHING AND THEY WILL GIVE ME A COOKIE T THE END....

WE TRIED TO GET OPAL TO HOLD SOMETHING INHER MOUTH AND ALL SHE DID WAS TO TRY AND HIDE HER HEAD.

WE ARE ALMOST BEHIND SCHEDULE FOR THE NEXT CALENDAR--

WHO'D A THUNK IT

****

THERE ARE SO MANY THINGS I SHOULD BE TEACHING THESE HOUSE DOGS OF MINE-- BENTLEY IS LOVELY--- BUT HE IS A SCATTERBRAINED NUT COMPARED TO THE OTHER STUDS I HAVE HAD-- AND IT IS ONLY BECAUSE I HAVE NOT SPENT TIME WITH HIM-- HE IS CAPABLE I DO BELIEVE

I SAY THAT BECAUSE---

I LET HIM OUT THE FRONT DOOR, TURNED AROUND TO PICK UP MY COFFEE- GOT ON MY GOLF CART (WITH VERY FEW BRAKES) AND RODE DOWN THO THE LAUNDRY BUILDING-

IN THAT AMOUNT OF TIME BENTLEY HAD GONE DOWN --
FLIPPED OPEN THE LATCH ON "HONEYMOON HILL" --
FLIPPED OPEN THE LATCH ON SCARLOTT'S KENNEL AND
WAS ACTIVELY ENGAGED IN PUPPY PRODUCTION BY THE
TIME I GOT THERE.

PROPERLY INSPIRED HE IS VERY CAPABLE..

****

THE 6 PUPS THAT DO NOT HAVE THIS "2 EXITS NO
WAITING" PROBLEM HAVE LOVELY STOOLS--

? TIME TO CLEAN UNDER THE STOVE AND FIGURE OUT
WHAT THEY ARE GETTING INTO ????

VOMITING IS ANOTHER THING DANES DO VERY WELL

Monday, September 2, 2013

daily doggie sept 2, 2013
i never saw getting into a bathrobe as any particular threat to my
health and well being... but last night- there were a bunch of
people in the living room and some Chinese food in the fridge.
since my jammies were not the most stylish i decided to put on the
bathrobe that had been hanging by the door for at least a year.

*when i was younger- by at least 6 months- i could cross my arms-
put them int he sleeve of my jacket and with a quick twist it would
land properly .*

*maybe i was younger then--- because the bathrobe did not land as
exspected ... instead the armpits landed, but the skirt did not clear
my head--- this is when i realized this bathrobe would fit a much
smaller person-- and i now had the problem of both arms held
straight up, and my head covered - because of my age (and wierd
shoulder joints) i could not get untangled.*

*i wear one of those "i have fallen and i can't get up" buttons- but
there is no way i was going to have the fire department arrive to
rescue me from this blindfolding bathrobe.- and the people in the
living room would never let me live it down...*

*i do not know who left thier bathrobe in my bedroom, but i had to
destroy it with scissors (and difficulty) to save myself.*

*you just never know when an event will remind you , you are not
74 any more.*

Tuesday, August 27, 2013

*FUNNY STORY THERE-- MARIA AND MEGAN CAME TO THE
TRACTOR TRAILER SITTING AT THE BOTTOM OF THE
DRIVEWAY AFRAID TO COME UP THE HILL FO R FEAR HE
COULD NOT TURN AROUND... HE SAID HE HAS BEEN TOLD
MANY TIMES HE COULD TURN THE 53 FOOT TRAILER IN
SOMEONE'S YARD ONLY TO HAVE TO BACK OUT.... SO I
DON'T KNWOW IF IT WAS MEGAN OR MARIA WHO SAID..
"WELL IF YOU CANT TURN IT AROUND, THERE IS A 75 YEAR
OLD WOMAN UP THERE in front of the teepee WHO WILL
TURN IT AROUND FOR YOU" --- GOTTA LOVE IT!!! HE CAME*

RIGHT IN THEN...

Tuesday, August 20, 2013

we have kenneling for 31 dogs and 3 litters--- plus any house dogs-
- for those of you who think i can not count...

and i am allowed one room and bath--

Sunday, August 3, 2013

WHICH BRINGS TO MIND.... AGE CAN HAVE AN
ADVANTAGE....

.WHEN I WS FIRST STARTING OUT WITH THIS SERVICE DOG
BIT, I KNEW I HAD PUBLIC ACCESS EITHER USING OR
TRAINING... THAT WAS THE LIMIT OF MY KNOWLEDGE.

IN A LOCAL MALL, ONE OF THOSE SECURITY TYPES WITH A
GUN, TOLD ME I HAD TO LEAVE- DOGS WERE NOT
ALLOWED IN THE MALL-- SO I PLAYED THE OLD LADY
WHO LEFT HER HEARING AID HOME AND JUST COULD
NOT UNDERSTAND ANYTHING-- SO I SAT DOWN-- SMILING..
I HAD 2 HOURS OF FUN WITH SECURITY AND VARIOUS
MALL MANAGERS.. THERE I SAT - SMILING WHILE THEY
TRIED TO FIGURE OUT WHAT WOULD SCARE ME INTO
MOVING...

.. NOTHING... I WAS READY TO PLEASENTLY DISRUPT
ANOTHER POLICE STATION IF THEY HAULED ME OFF...
THEY EVENTUALYY GAVE UP...

July, 2012

*SO, the police called 4:30 am   to ask if all our horses are accounted for--- they had one running down rt 97 --- and rather than go look, I grabbed a metal bucket and some oats, grabbed an emergency rope (hanging by the door where it should be!) the trailer was hooked (thank heavens and **shep)** - so i took it-- and went to rt 97... i waltzed in (in my pajamas) made a metal noise with the oats in the bucket - and the galloping horse stopped, and walked right up me and stuck his head in the bucket-- and was well trained so i could easily control him with that emergency rope deal-- in less than 30 seconds I had fixed what the police had been chasing all night.*

once i had the rope around it's neck, i bent down to see if it had testicles, because if it did i only had 23 seconds until it finished the small quantity of oats before all hell could break loose.-- there is a inverse relationship between food and testosterone in many species

the police made all the blue lights flash while i loaded the horse on the trailer... made an illegal u turn under the blue lights-- and came home.

So we now have someone's big red horse..-- i am sure it is not ours--- it looks just like the red chestnut mare we have (who is ?800 pounds?)?   -- except this horse is big..?1200 pounds???

i saw no reason to unload her--- and am waiting for the police to call back with the owner's name.. and i am trying to get janine to be sure she did not put one like this in our barn... pretty horse....but far too fat. Its now 8:30 am and the horse is still here?

MERRY CHRISTMAS - DECEMBER 25, 2012
fleeting thru my head are topics being chased by the "you can't put that in an email

****

there is a scotish poem about that ... fortunately i can't remember it all

but the concept is---- change happens...

i started in a story- then i stopped it in the middle

for the story that i started was not, you see,

the kind that you could tell at a church party

i forgot the middle part.. but it goes on....

and many years had passed when fortune gave me such a shock

when the ministers youngest daughter at her fathers jubilee

told the story that i started at the church party.

****

the british have a much more amusing way with words than americans..

highly recommended are the stanley halloway monologues

if you can deal with the accent-- the cd-- otherwise get the book

i do know the full albert and the lion-- but i will spare you-

****

we --- earlene and i -- are anxiously awaiting the arrival of ginger from atlanta-- a camera person who's christmas present from her husband in Afghanistan was to come here and pick poops for a week and stay in the guest house......

she has to be one of the chosen --

when i got up -- willow was in the chair and earlene on the floor.-- whatever-- they are quiet...... at the moment

****

the point to ponder today-- in my opinion....

the yuppy puppy training--- for th 47th time i explained to someone,,, i have never been able to train a dog using my muscles.. historically--- i tried to teach a dog to roll over by rolling hm over-- 3 days later the dog had learned nothing- but i realized they don't learn that way..

and that sure pertains to the yuppy puppies--- the instinct to pick up the foot and put it on the lever is great-- but the minute you extend the leg the dog begins to pull back- and all the concentration is on getting their foot away from you and they never learn to push the lever.

and then (this is the exciting part...) that concept pertains to 99% of the training we do... you might have to use a muscle to start th etraiing.... cause something to happen then instantly release the dog to let them think about it.

****

this is my tight leash lesson- pull them sharply into place next to you then totally relax the leash- let them think-- if they pull - do it again- before too many the dog will stand next to you. at that point you are well on your way to a trained dog-- do the same thing while walking...

walk next to me on a loose leash or you will get put back in place with that thing around your neck-(which preferably should be a plain chain ' training collar)-

that is nearly the same concept as using my muscles to get the paw on the yuppy puppy lever-- it is the stop and let them think which trains them

***

i took on a bet at a Sunday stew--- an absolutely impossible pit bull - the owners couldn't even get him out of the car... they had been told the harness would help them control the dog.. mistake-- those things teach the dogs to pull.. any rate.. i put on one of our training collars and

politely said to the dog"let me explain it to you"

--a couple "oh no you don't"

and he stood at my feet with a " that is not what usually happens" look on his face.

we walked off to the t-tent with him on a loose leash-- i told him to lie down at my feet- and he did- perfect behavior

then i had to try and train th eowner... that did n't go as well...

****

pups think it is time to gt out and play with the boxes from yesterdays ups delivery.. kongs--- canned food treat food- cookies-- coffee--cardboard-- checks-- and shampoo -- thanks to one and all-

and the calendars are nearly sold out (1000 of them) and the jan food and oil bill chicken sh#t wall are nearly all gone too...

tis the season...

ABOUT THE AUTHOR

Janine Jacques, MBA, MSCIS, PH.D

Associate Professor, New England College of Business in Boston. She is
the founder of Hope4Horses and the Equine Rescue Network.. Janine is
active with the Service Dog Project, rides her two horses infrequently
(Crosby and Lincoln), and lives happily in Boxford, Massachusetts with her
son Colby and Thumper, the big black dog.

Made in the USA
Lexington, KY
23 October 2013